# The Kurds in Turkey

# The Kurds in Turkey

## A Political Dilemma

Michael M. Gunter

**Westview Press**

BOULDER • SAN FRANCISCO • OXFORD

*Westview Special Studies on the Middle East*

This Westview softcover edition is printed on acid-free paper and bound in library-quality, coated covers that carry the highest rating of the National Association of State Textbook Administrators, in consultation with the Association of American Publishers and the Book Manufacturers' Institute.

Copyright © 1990 by Westview Press, Inc.

Published in 1990 in the United States of America by Westview Press, Inc., 5500 Central Avenue, Boulder, Colorado 80301, and in the United Kingdom by Westview Press, 36 Lonsdale Road, Summertown, Oxford OX2 7EW

Library of Congress Cataloging-in-Publication Data
Gunter, Michael M.
  The Kurds in Turkey: a political dilemma / Michael M.
  Gunter
    p. cm. — (Westview special studies on the Middle East)
  Includes bibliographical references and index.
  ISBN 0-8133-8120-7
  1. Kurds—Turkey, Eastern—Politics and government. 2. Kurds—
Civil rights—Turkey, Eastern. 3. Turkey—Politics and
government—1960–1980. 4. Turkey—Politics and government—1980–
5. Turkey, Eastern—Ethnic relations. I. Title. II. Series.
DS51.E27G86 1990
323.1′191590561—dc20
                                   90-42499
                                     CIP

Printed and bound in the United States of America

The paper used in this publication meets the requirements
of the American National Standard for Permanence of Paper
for Printed Library Materials Z39.48-1984.

10   9   8   7   6   5   4   3   2

# Contents

# Acknowledgments

I would like to thank the Non-Instructional Faculty Assignment Committee at Tennessee Technological University for giving me a semester of released time during which I was able to write much of this book. Angelo Volpe, the President of Tennessee Tech, encouraged and supported me, for which I am very grateful. Robert Bode, Steve Khleif, and Paul Stephenson gave me a considerable amount of help in the mechanics of word processing, while Sanford Silverburg and Steve Tabachnick have been sources of academic encouragement for many years. In writing this book I also have had the benefit of advice from Michael Turner, Heath Lowry, Vera Beaudin Saeedpour, Siyamend Othman, Jennifer Noyon, Paul Henze, and Mehmet Ali Birand, as well as others who have preferred to remain anonymous.

My year spent as a Senior Fulbright Lecturer in International Relations at the Middle East Technical University in Ankara, Turkey, first sensitized me to the issues I have analyzed here. The Fulbright Program was a marvelous broadening experience for me. I hope such academic exchanges will always be supported, for they pay such rich dividends in international understanding and peace.

I thank *The Middle East Journal* and *Conflict Quarterly* for giving me permission to use material that appeared in earlier articles I published in them. Special thanks go to Michael S. Miller for permission to use the excellent map he drew of the Kurdish minority in Turkey. Finally, I would like to mention that I omitted the diacritical marks in foreign words to simplify the text; the meanings of the words have not been affected.

*Michael M. Gunter*

# THE KURDISH MINORITY OF TURKEY

0   50   100
miles

Black Sea

GEORGIA    Tbilisi

■ Batumi

SOVIET

UNION

Ordu

Giresun    Trabzon    ● Rize    Qoruh

Kars

Tokat    Gumushane    ARMENIA
Yerevan

Sivas    Erzincan    Erzurum    ●Agri

■ Ulas    Tunceli    ■ Maku

Hozat    Karakocan    Bingol    Mus    IRAN

Elazig    Bitlis    L. Van    Van

Malatya    Diyarbakir    Siirt

Adiyaman    Gercus    Sirnak    Hakkari

Maras    Mardin    Semdinli

Gaziantep    Urfa    Derik    Nusaybin    ■ Zakho

Kilis    ■ Al Qamishli    Duhok    IRAQ

SYRIA    Al Hasakah

---

### KEY to MAIN MAP

Odessa    SOVIET    UNION

ROMANIA    0    500    1000
miles    N

BULG.    Istanbul    Tbilisi

Ankara    Area of
TURKEY    Detail

GREECE    SYRIA    Tehran

LEBANON    Baghdad
ISRAEL

Cairo ■    JORD.    IRAQ    AFGHAN

EGYPT    SAUDI    IRAN
ARABIA

LIBYA    Riyadh    OMAN

SUDAN

● Provincial Capital
(Provinces take name
of capital town)

■ Other Town

Provinces under
State of Emergency

Provinces with Large
Kurdish population:

20 - 60%    More than
of Total    60% of Total

© 1988 Michael S. Miller

# Introduction

The Kurds are a Sunni Muslim, Indo-European-speaking people whose traditional homeland is concentrated in the rugged, mountainous area of the Middle East where Turkey, Iraq, and Iran converge. Much smaller numbers also inhabit Syria and the Soviet Union, while a diaspora has now spread to several other Mideastern states as well as western Europe and North America. Although they constitute the fourth largest ethnic group in the Middle East, the Kurds lack their own independent state. As such, they are one of the largest ethnic groups in the world thus situated.

A number of useful studies of the Kurds exist.[1] Very few, however, deal specifically with those living in Turkey.[2] This dearth of analysis is ironic since approximately half of the Kurds in the world live in Turkey. What is more, in the past few years a long-festering disaffection for the Turkish state on the part of some of them has developed into a small, but sustained guerrilla war in southeastern Anatolia. Commenting on what it termed the "persistence of Kurdish separatism" in eastern Turkey, an assessment by the United States Central Intelligence Agency (CIA) stated:

> The Kurds' sense of separate identity has not been significantly reduced by the [Turkish] government's attempts to co-opt or suppress them. The Kurdish language has flourished, and clandestinely published Kurdish literature is surreptitiously obtainable in Kurdish areas. . . . In the past several years, several overt "cultural associations" and covert liberation groups have formed to promote the idea of Kurdish autonomy and independence.[3]

*1*

In an editorial entitled "Something's going on in east Turkey," the chairman and founder of the *Turkish Daily News*, Ilhan Cevik, added:

> There is no doubt left now that the situation in the region is extremely serious. The Turkish armed forces units there are in a state of permanent alert and security operations are going on round the clock. According to official statements bands of separatist terrorists are being harbored and trained in some neighboring countries. The insurgents are involved in all manner of activities in the region and despite the extensive security measures they are still very active. . . . As a matter of fact they regularly raid military patrols, gendarmerie stations and even prisons.[4]

The purpose of this study is to analyze the current Kurdish problem in Turkey from the point of view of the Turkish authorities and their supporters, as well as from the perspective of disaffected Kurds living in that state and abroad. Analyzed specifically will be the historical background to this situation, the political instability and terrorism rampant in Turkey during the late 1970s, the legal suppression of the Kurds, the emergence of numerous Kurdish political parties in the 1970s of which the *Partia Karkaren Kurdistan* (PKK) or Kurdish Workers Party has been the most noteworthy, the current activities of the PKK, and transnational influences on the situation. Finally, some tentative conclusions will be offered. My hope is to throw some objective light on a troubling problem that has been poorly understood.

### Notes

1. For two excellent examples, see Thomas Bois and Vladimir Minorsky, "Kurds, Kurdistan," *The Encyclopedia of Islam* (new edition), V, 1981, 438-486; and M. M. van Bruinessen, *Agha, Shaikh and State: On the Social and Political Organization of Kurdistan* (Utrecht, The Netherlands: University of Utrecht, 1978). In addition, see such recent studies as David McDowall, *The Kurds*, Report No. 23 (London: Minority Rights Group Ltd., 1985); Anthony Hyman, *Elusive Kurdistan: The Struggle for Recognition*, No. 214 (London: The Centre for Security and Conflict Studies, 1988); and Charles G. MacDonald, "The Kurdish Question in the 1980s," in *Ethnicity, Pluralism, and the State in the Middle East*, ed. by Milton J. Esman and Itamar Rabinovich (Ithaca: Cornell University Press, 1988), pp. 233-252.

2. I am aware of two excellent exceptions in English to this general statement. See Kendal [Nezan], "Kurdistan in Turkey," in *People without a Country: The Kurds and Kurdistan*, ed. by Gerard Chaliand (London: Zed Press, 1980), pp. 47-106; and Martin van Bruinessen, "The Kurds in Turkey," *MERIP Reports*, No. 121 (Feb. 1984), pp. 6-12.

3. National Foreign Assessment Center (U.S. Central Intelligence Agency), *The Kurdish Problem in Perspective* (Aug. 1979). The research for this study was done by analysts from the Office of Political Analysis and the Office of Geographic and Cartographic Research, and coordinated within the CIA. Although it was stamped "secret," it was seized during the occupation of the U.S. Embassy in Tehran during 1979. In citing from it, I am simply conveying information that is now in the public domain. In no way, do I condone the method by which it became thus available. Throughout my ensuing text, I refer to this analysis as the "CIA Report."

4. Ilhan Cevik, "Something's going on in east Turkey," *Turkish Daily News*, Nov. 11, 1985, p. 5.

# 1

## Background

### Origins

The origin of the Kurds is uncertain, although many scholars believe them to be the descendants of various Indo-European tribes which settled in the area as many as 4000 years ago. The Kurds themselves claim to be the descendants of the Medes who overthrew Nineveh in 612 B.C., and also recite interesting myths about their origins involving King Solomon, jinni, and other magical agents.[1] Many believe that the Kardouchoi, who gave Xenophon and his 10,000 such a mauling as they retreated from Persia in 400 B.C., were the ancestors of the Kurds.

In the seventh century A.D., the conquering Arabs applied the name "Kurds" to the mountainous people they Islamicized in the region, and history records that the famous Saladin, who fought against Richard the Lionheart and the Christian Crusaders so successfully in the twelfth century, was a Kurd.

### Divisions

Whatever their exact origin, it is clear that racially the Kurds today constitute a mixture of various groupings, the result of earlier invasions and migrations.[2] What is more, it should be noted that, although the Indo-European Kurdish language is an important element of the Kurdish culture, it too is divided into three major dialects (Kurdi, Kurmanji, and Zara), the first two of which are further split into distinct subdialects. The Turkish Kurds use the

Kurmanji and Zara dialects which are, for the most part, mutually unintelligible.

Tribalism too has prevented Kurdish unity. Indeed, it is probably true that the tribe has received more loyalty than any sense of Kurdish nationalism. In all of the Kurdish revolts of the twentieth century, for example--whether in Turkey, Iraq, or Iran--significant numbers of Kurds have supported the government because of their tribal antipathies for those rebelling. Similarly, the aghas (feudal landlords or tribal chieftains) and sheikhs (religious leaders) continue to command allegiances inconsistent with the full development of a modern sense of nationalism.

Although most Turkish Kurds are Sunni Muslims of the Shafii jurisprudence (in contrast to the Turks of Turkey who are Sunni Muslims of the Hanefite school) many Kurds are attracted to various Dervish orders whose differences tend further to divide them. In addition, a significant number of Turkish Kurds adhere to an unorthodox form of Shiism and in Turkey are referred to as "Alevis."[3]

## Population

The Kurdish population in Turkey constitutes a majority in the following southeastern Anatolian provinces which border on or are located near Syria, Iraq, and Iran: Mardin, Siirt, Hakkari, Diyarbakir, Bitlis, Mus, Van, and Agri. In addition, significant numbers also live in the contiguous provinces of Urfa, Adiyaman, Malatya, Elazig, Tunceli, Erzincan, Bingol, and Kars. Because of deportations and more voluntary migrations, some also live in various other parts of Turkey such as Istanbul.

No precise or even reliable estimate of the Kurdish population exists, however. Over zealous Kurds claim figures as high as 26,000,000 with 12,000,000 of these being in Turkey alone.[4] Another Kurdish source in 1975 claimed that 10.5 million Kurds live in Turkey,[5] while more recent ones contended that the figure now was either 11 million[6] or 12 million.[7] The Kurdish author Kendal (Nezan) wrote that "there were about 8.5 million Kurdish speakers in 1970, which represents 23.8% of the population." He then admitted, however, that because of the inherent difficulties involved, "this figure . . . is probably not very accurate."[8]

On the other hand, the states in which Kurds live probably undercount them for obvious political reasons. The Turkish census of

1965 was the last one to include questions concerning the mother tongue. This indicated that 8 percent of the population might be considered Kurdish and was the resident majority in eight of the southeastern provinces.[9] It is clear, however, that some Kurds would not have wanted to list Kurdish as their mother tongue or considered Turkish to be so. No census since then has sought to determine the Kurdish population in Turkey. As Kendal has observed: "Turkish authorities prefer to minimize the numbers, whilst some nationalist groups tend to exaggerate them."[10]

Although the U.S. CIA estimated that in 1979 there were approximately "4 to 6 million [Kurds] in Turkey," a figure which represented only "approximately 10 percent" of the total population,[11] and the veteran British press observer of Turkey, David Barchard, wrote in 1985 "of perhaps 6-8 million Kurds,"[12] others indicate that the actual total is probably higher. The Turkish weekly, *Briefing*, for example, declared in 1989 that "Turkey's Kurdish population [was] believed to be over 8 million."[13] Berch Berberoglu has asserted that it is closer to 20 percent,[14] a figure with which David McDowall,[15] Richard Sims,[16] and the careful authority on the Kurds, Martin van Bruinessen,[17] basically agreed. Another recent (1987) estimate of the Kurdish population in Turkey, however, was somewhat less: 9,000,000.[18]

In partial explanation for these widely differing population estimates one should note that, given the assimilation into Turkish society undergone by many Kurds, it is not unreasonable for the Turkish government to consider "Turkish," many whom others might call "Kurdish." Ismet Inonu, the famous Turkish lieutenant of and successor to Mustafa Kemal Ataturk, for example, was possibly an ethnic Kurd.[19] If he was, however, it did not prevent him from taking a strong Turkish nationalist position against Kurdish claims. Referring to the Kurdish uprisings in eastern Turkey during the 1920s, for example, Inonu declared: "Only the Turkish nation is entitled to claim ethnic and national rights in this country. No other element has any such right."[20]

Ziya Gokalp, the most famous theoretician of modern Turkish nationalism, was of Kurdish origins. This, however, did not prevent him from penning the famous couplet: "The country of the Turks is not Turkey, nor yet Turkistan. Their country is a vast and eternal land: Turan!"[21] Other prominent Turks of possible Kurdish backgrounds include: former Presidents Fahri Koruturk and Cevdet Sunay, former Prime Minister Ferit Melen, and the current (since November 1989) President and former Prime Minister, Turgut Ozal.[22] In modern Turkey there can be no doubt that a significant number of historically ethnic Kurds have been completely assimilated into Turkish society and no longer even speak Kurdish.

The Turks came late to the idea of a nation-state, but after it had helped to destroy their multinational Ottoman Empire following World War I and even threatened the very existence of their Anatolian heartland, they too learned to value one for themselves. David Barchard suggests that "the proportion of urban and middle-class Turks whose grandparents came as refugees from the Balkans, Crete, Egypt, the Caucasus or other parts of the Soviet Union is probably well over 50 percent."[23] The modern Republic of Turkey itself was only established after a long and terrible struggle against the invading Greeks in the west, a lesser but still serious one against the Armenians in the east, and the diplomatic victory at Lausanne under which the victorious allies of World War I recognized the new situation. Nurtured on the Kemalist ideology of Republican Turkey's national unity and territorial integrity which had sprung from this earlier trauma of the gradual disintegration of the Ottoman Empire, the Turkish hesitancy to bolster artificially the number of Kurds in Turkey today can be readily appreciated. On the other hand, the claim by some that the Turkish Kurds are really "mountain Turks" who have forgotten their Turkish origins is as intellectually bankrupt as the now discredited theory of the "Sun Language," which maintained that the origin of all languages was Turkish.

## Notes

1. See, for example, C. J. Edmonds, *Kurds, Turks and Arabs: Politics, Travel and Research in North-Eastern Iraq 1919-1925* (London: Oxford University Press, 1957), p. 4. Margaret Kahn entitled her delightful account of life among the Iranian Kurds, *Children of the Jinn: In Search of the Kurds and Their Country* (New York: Seaview Books, 1980).

2. For a detailed analysis of the Kurds' complicated and heterogeneous ethnic makeup, see Vladimir Minorsky, "Kurds," *The Encyclopaedia of Islam*, II, 1927, 1132-1155.

3. For an excellent analysis of these linguistic, tribal, and religious differences among the Turkish Kurds, see, in general, M.M. van Bruinessen,

*Agha, Shaikh and State: On the Social and Political Organization of Kurdistan* (Utrecht, The Netherlands: University of Utrecht, 1978).

4. *Azadi Kurdistan Humane Foundation* (South San Francisco, California), Mar. 1986, p. 1.

5. "Kurdistan of Turkey," *DRUK* (Defend the Rights of United Kurdistan), Bulletin No. 3, Vol. 1, July 30, 1975.

6. Boug Lana, "The Socio-Economic Framework of National Oppression in Kurdistan-Turkey," *The Kurdish Culture Bulletin* 1 (Nov. 1988), p. 20.

7. B. Jaff, "Northern Kurdistan: The Growing Turmoil," *The Kurdish Observer*, Feb. 1987, p. 14.

8. Kendal [Nezan], "Kurdistan in Turkey," in *People without a Country: The Kurds and Kurdistan*, ed. by Gerard Chaliand (London: Zed Press, 1980), p. 48.

9. Dankwart A. Rustow, *Turkey: America's Forgotten Ally* (New York: Council on Foreign Relations, 1987), p. 37.

10. Kendal, "Kurdistan in Turkey," p. 48.

11. National Foreign Assessment Center (U.S. Central Intelligence Agency), *The Kurdish Problem in Perspective* (Aug. 1979), p. 8.

12. David Barchard, *Turkey and the West* (London: Routledge & Kegan Paul for the Royal Institute of International Affairs, 1985), p. 13.

13. "Problems Prevail As the Winter Sets In," *Briefing*, Sept. 18, 1989, p. 15.

14. Berch Berberoglu, *Turkey in Crisis* (London: Zed Press, 1982), p. 126n.50.

15. David McDowall, *The Kurds*, Report No. 23 (London: Minority Rights Group, Ltd., 1985), p. 7.

16. Richard Sims, *Kurdistan: The Search for Recognition*, Conflict Study No. 124 (London: The Institute for the Study of Conflict, 1980), p. 3.

17. Bruinessen, *Agha, Shaikh and State*, p. 12.

18. Anthony Hyman, *Elusive Kurdistan: The Struggle for Recognition*, Conflict Study No. 214 (London: The Centre for Security and Conflict Studies, 1988), p. 4.

19. Although Inonu's possible Kurdish heritage is seldom mentioned in any sources, see Edgar O'Ballance, *The Kurdish Revolt: 1961-1970* (Hamden, Conn.: Archon Books, 1973), p. 28.

20. *Milliyet*, No. 1636, Aug. 31, 1930, as cited in Kendal, "Kurdistan in Turkey," p. 65.

21. Cited in Bernard Lewis, *The Emergence of Modern Turkey* (London: Oxford University Press, 1968), p. 351.

22. Adnan Kahveci, "On the Question of Ethnic Problems in Turkey," *Turkish Daily News*, June 2, 1987, p. 6.

23. Barchard, *Turkey and the West*, p. 13.

# 2

## Prelude to Conflict

Early in the sixteenth century most of the Kurds loosely fell under Ottoman rule, while the remainder were placed under the Persians.[1] According to the Kurdish authority Kendal, "over fifty insurrections . . . broke out during the [nineteenth] century" in response to the Porte's attempt to impose his authority over the Kurds more thoroughly.[2] Sheikh Obeidullah's revolt in 1880, probably represented "the first indication of Kurdish political nationalism. . . . [It] aimed at uniting the Kurdish peoples of the Turkish and Persian empires into one state, but . . . failed when both empires cooperated to eliminate the common threat."[3]

In 1891, Sultan Abdulhamid II created the Hamidiye, a Kurdish cavalry that, according to Robert Olson, was used as part of a policy "to try to establish central authority . . . [and] greater Muslim unity."[4] The Hamidiye were also used against the Armenians in a policy of divide and rule. Given the training its officers received and its exposure to nationalistic ideas while serving in eastern Anatolia and the Balkans, Olson has concluded that "the Hamidiye were an important stage in the emergence of Kurdish nationalism from 1891 to 1914."[5] Despite the influences of the Young Turk Revolution of 1908 and the tremendous devastation that occurred in eastern Anatolia during World War I, however, the Kurds of southeastern Anatolia still maintained a traditionalist position of supporting the Caliphate as represented by the Ottoman Sultan.

During World War I, one of U.S. President Wilson's Fourteen Points (Number 12) declared that the non-Turkish minorities of the Ottoman Empire should be granted the right of "autonomous development." The stillborn Treaty of Sevres signed in August 1920 provided for "local autonomy for the predominantly Kurdish areas" (Article 62) and in Article 64 even looked forward to the possibility that "the Kurdish peoples" might be granted "independence from Turkey." Turkey's quick revival under Mustafa Kemal (Ataturk)-- ironically enough with considerable Kurdish help as the Turks played well on the theme of Islamic unity--altered the entire situation. The subsequent and definitive Treaty of Lausanne in July 1923 recognized the modern Republic of Turkey without any special provisions for the Turkish Kurds.

When Mustafa Kemal (Ataturk) first began to form a Turkish nation-state after World War I, it was not clear what constituted a Turk.[6] Thus, Ismet (Inonu's) initial formula of modern Turkey as a "homeland of Kurds and Turks"[7] might be seen as an unsuccessful attempt to define the term. Soon, however, it was abandoned in favor of a broader definition that included the Kurds as Turks. Given the inchoate fluidity of ethnic consciousness in the Islamic world and the perceived need of political unity, one could argue that such a definition of "Turkish" made sense and was not unreasonable.

Mustafa Kemal's creation of a secular and purely Turkish state, however, altered the situation. From 1925 to 1939, there were three major revolts by the Turkish Kurds: (1) the rising in 1925 of Sheikh Said, the hereditary chief of the powerful Nakhshvandi Dervish sect; (2) the insurrection led by Khoybun (Independence) under General Ihsan Nuri Pasha in the Ararat area in 1930; and finally (3) the Dersim (now called Tunceli) rebellion led by Sheikh Sayyid Rida from 1936 to the end of 1938. All were completely crushed by the vastly superior Turkish military,[8] and from then on the Turkish Kurds were, until the 1970s, largely quiescent.

Describing what had occurred, Bruinessen wrote that "in Turkey . . . after the great Kurdish nationalist revolts . . . a systematic policy aiming at detribalization and assimilation of the Kurds was adopt- ed. . . . Everything that recalled a separate Kurdish identity was to be abolished: language, clothing, names."[9] The Turkish Kurds had become "mountain Turks."

The Kurdish authority Kendal put it much more harshly:

During these thirteen years of repression, struggle, revolt, and deportation . . . more than *one and a half million* [emphasis in the original] Kurds were deported and massacred. . . . The entire area beyond the Euphrates . . . was declared out of bounds to foreigners until 1965 and was kept under a permanent state of siege till 1950. The use of the Kurdish language was banned. The very words "Kurd" and "Kurdistan" were crossed out of the dictionaries and history books. The Kurds were never even referred to except as "Mountain Turks."[10]

This apparent implication that 1.5 million Kurds might have been massacred would seem to be a gross exaggeration.  L. Rambout, for example, wrote indignantly that after the 1925 revolt 206 villages were destroyed, 8,758 houses burned, and 15,200 people killed.[11] McDowall opined vaguely that "anything between 40,000 and 250,000, died in the pacification" and that "perhaps over one million Kurds were forcibly displaced between 1925-1938."[12] Given such a wide variance in these figures and their obvious polemical intentions, Bruinessen's simple conclusion that "many Kurds were exiled to other parts of the country"[13] would seem to be a more objective viewpoint.

In analyzing the results of the unsuccessful Kurdish revolts in Turkey, Kendal argued further that these actions "were shored up by a mythical Turkish history" that claimed:

the Kurds were of Turanian [Turkic] origin. . . . If they now spoke a 'dialect,' which was nothing but a 'mixture of old Turkish, Persian, Arabic and Armenian,' this was due to the fact that 'lost in their inaccessible mountains, the Kurds ended up by forgetting their mother tongue'. . . . It was this fantastic, aggressive and exaggerated nationalism which confronted the Kurdish people.[14]

The CIA assessment of the situation gave some credence to Kendal's analyses when it stated:

In the early days of the Turkish Republic, the government responded to Kurdish protests against Ataturk's modernizing and centralizing reforms by ruthlessly suppressing all antigovernmental activity and by attempting, albeit unsuccessfully, to eliminate all manifestations of Kurdish culture and nationalism.[15]

In July 1943, another Kurdish sheikh in Turkey, Said Biroki, briefly led a few tribes in rebellion against the Turkish government. He attacked police and frontier posts and demanded autonomy, but within a matter of weeks was captured and his forces dispersed.

At the end of World War II, *Razgar i Kurd* (Kurdish Deliverance), a loosely organized, short-lived coalition of Kurdish groups in Iraq, attempted to keep the Kurdish cause in Turkey alive by sending a virulent appeal to the new United Nations organization.

> During the past 25 years the Kurds have and are suffering severely under the tyrannical regime of Turkey. . . . It is indeed misfortune that the world is on the threshold of peace and many conferences are held to discuss and solve the world problems, and the Kurds in Turkey are unable to have their voice heard in these conferences. . . . In view of such a calamitous and hopeless situation our Party demands that this criminal Kemalist gang which calls itself a government be removed and the Kurdish people given its full natural rights and full opportunity to self-determination.[16]

Nothing, of course, came of this appeal since the obvious purpose of the Turkish government was to make the Turkish Kurds not only politically Turks (as legally they already were), but also culturally and socially Turks through assimilation. A number of constitutional and legal provisions, described below in Chapter 4, were devised to promote this ban on the Kurdish culture and language.

On the other hand, to the extent that Turkish Kurds conform to the constitutional order, they are free to participate fully in Turkish society since they are Turkish citizens. Over the years, therefore, the Turkish Kurds have wielded real electoral power, while some of them have risen to prestigious positions in Turkish government and society. The government also makes a genuine attempt to integrate Kurdish students into the more established universities in the western part of the country and does not seriously try to prevent the Kurdish language from being spoken privately. Given the rudimentary sense of ethnic consciousness in the Islamic world when the Turkish Republic was first established, the continuing perceived need of political unity, as well as the fact that over the years a significant number of historically ethnic Kurds have been completely assimilated into Turkish society and no longer even speak Kurdish--the Turkish policy towards its Kurdish population can be understood, if not necessarily condoned.

## The Situation after 1950

According to most accounts, the institution of multiparty democracy in Turkey in 1950 enabled the Kurds to improve their situation.[17]

All Turkish citizens were entitled to vote, and it became possible for Kurdish voters in the east to wield real electoral power. The Democrat Party of the new prime minister, Adnan Menderes, in particular, took pains to win the support of this lucrative following.

After the military coup of May 27, 1960, the deposed Menderes claimed that a number of Kurdish politicians had used their positions of power in an attempt to achieve Kurdish independence. Although this accusation was probably exaggerated, the new military government arrested some 485 Kurds in June 1960 and detained them for several months. The 55 most influential were exiled to western Turkey for two years; all but one of them had been members of Menderes' party.[18]

Meanwhile, according to Kendal, the new military government had begun to intensify "the Turkicization of the names of Kurdish villages and towns."[19] In April 1961, General Cemal Gursel, the leader of the junta, lauded a book written by Sherif Firat who claimed that the Kurds were Turkish in origin. The Turkish leader went on to declare that eastern Anatolia was both "gate and fortress" whose loss would threaten the Turkish ability to maintain their position to the west.[20] In May 1961, demonstrations apparently took place in Mardin, Deykir, Siverek, Diyarbakir, Bitlis, and Van. Kurds carried signs which declared: "We are not Turks, we are Kurds," "Down with Guersel, Menderes, Inonu--All tyrants," "The Turkish Government must recognize our national rights."[21]

Despite the unrest, the new Turkish constitution of 1961 granted considerably more civil liberties involving speech, press, and association than had previously existed. Although the ban on forming any regional or ethnic associations that might impair Turkish unity was maintained, the Turkish Kurds still benefitted from these new freedoms. A Kurd from Diyarbakir, Dr. Yusuf Azizoglu, became one of the leaders of the New Turkey Party. For a brief period in 1962, he was the minister of health in the new Inonu government. In this position he built a number of hospitals and dispensaries in the east until forced to resign amid charges of "regionalism."

The Turkish press also began cautiously examining the Kurdish problem. *Baris Dunyasi* (World of Peace), a liberal Turkish journal, began publishing some articles by Musa Anter on the Kurdish language, literature, and folklore in 1962. In September of that year *Dicle-Firat* (Tigris-Euphrates), a bilingual monthly in Turkish and Kurdish, appeared in Istanbul. It was banned after a few issues, but other journals such as *Dicle Kaynagi* (Origin of the Tigris), *Deng* (Voice), and *Riya Newe* (New Path) took its place. They too, however, were eventually banned.

At the same time, the Turkish press began extended coverage of the Kurdish uprising in Iraq that was led by Mullah Mustafa Barzani, a traditionalist and nationalist. No doubt the example of the Iraqi Kurdish movement encouraged many Turkish Kurds. Indeed, in 1965, a Kurdish Democratic Party of Turkey (KDPT) was created by Faik Bucak, a Kurdish lawyer from Urfa and member of the Turkish parliament, on the model of Barzani's Kurdish Democratic Party (KDP).

While the leftist Kurdish movements of this time in Turkey spoke only about cultural rights and economic equality, the aim of the KDPT, which drew its supporters mainly from the traditional Kurdish elite, was autonomy or even independence. After Bucak was murdered in the late 1960s, the party underwent a number of splits. Dr. Shivan established his more radical, populist faction and, with some followers, withdrew to Iraq where he began to make plans for armed attacks across the Turkish border.

After the Turkish military intervention of 1971, the rival KDPT and its leader Sait Elchi, also fled to Iraq. There under circumstances which remain obscure, both Elchi and Shivan were killed, and the activities of their organizations came to an end. Martin van Bruinessen has written that Shivan apparently killed Elchi and then was himself executed by Barzani. Bruinessen added, however, that Kurdish sources explained what had occurred as provocation by the Turkish intelligence service, the MIT.[22]

The Turkish left legally emerged in the 1960s under the guise of the Turkish Workers Party (TWP) and in the 1965 elections won 15 seats. Gradually the TWP took an interest in the Kurdish question and at its fourth congress in October 1970 passed a remarkable resolution that stated: "There is a Kurdish people in the East of Turkey. . . . The fascist authorities representing the ruling classes have subjected the Kurdish people to a policy of assimilation and intimidation which has often become a bloody repression."[23]

In the context of Turkish politics, this was a unique proclamation. Never before had a legal political party represented in the Turkish parliament recognized explicitly the existence of a Kurdish people in Turkey. In June 1971, however, the new military-backed government that had come to power earlier that year dissolved the TWP and sentenced its main leaders to prison, in part, for advocating pro-Kurdish, separatist activities.

Because explicitly Kurdish societies remained illegal, many Kurds naturally gravitated toward revolutionary leftist movements and became disproportionately represented in them. Indeed, Deniz Gezmis and Mahir Cayan, arguably the two most renowned of the radical Turkish youth in these years, were both Kurds. Although they spoke openly of "a Kurdish people" and virtually incited the Kurds in eastern Turkey to secede, Gezmis and Cayan were clearly Marxist radicals first before being Kurdish nationalists. Cayan became famous as the leader of the Turkish Peoples Liberation Party and Front (THKP-C), while Gezmis won similar status as the leader of the Turkish Peoples Liberation Army (THKO). Both were killed in 1972: Gezmis was executed for murder and Cayan died in a shootout with Turkish army commandos.

Cayan believed that the Turkish masses were being controlled by a civilian-military oligarchy that had silenced them by imposing an "artificial balance" of power maintained by force and fear. Through "armed propaganda," i. e. armed violence, he would disrupt the state's "artificial balance" and force the Turkish government to show its true fascist face. Once this occurred, even the landlords with national feelings and the industrialists who opposed the imperialist takeover of their property would join the masses of people in a successful revolutionary action. During the 1970s, some twenty different terrorist groups claimed to follow Cayan's ideology.

Still another Kurdish leftist during these years, Ibrahim Kaypakkaya, headed a military flank called the Turkish Workers-Peasants Liberation Army (TIKKO) which in time established a political structure termed the Turkish Communist Party-Marxist Leninist (TKP-ML). Kaypakkaya too was killed in the early 1970s, although TIKKO went on to play a major role in the terrorist violence that plagued Turkey before the military coup in September 1980. Supposedly destroyed by the new military government, it returned to the scene in the late 1980s.

The freedom of the 1960s also encouraged extreme rightists such as Colonel Alparslan Turkes' pan-Turkic Nationalist Action Party. With his armed militia, Turkes was able violently to express his hostility not only toward "leftists," but the Kurds too.[24]

On August 3, 1967, Kurdish "national committees" in Diyarbakir and other cities in eastern Turkey issued manifestoes condemning the

Turkish government of Suleyman Demirel for ignoring their educational and economic needs.[25] Mass rallies were held in Diyarbakir and Silvan. Although the word "Kurd" was not even mentioned at these meetings, the implications were clear, especially since the participation was so broadly based. In addition to the local Kurdish intellectuals and professionals, for example, there also were tribal leaders, landlords, urban craftsmen, workers, and peasants present. New demonstrations broke out in eastern Turkey in 1968.

The following year (1969), Kurdish intellectuals in Ankara and Istanbul, and then in eastern Turkey established the first legal Kurdish organization, the Revolutionary Cultural Society of the East, or the DDKO (its Turkish acronym). Many of its leaders were also members of the TWP. In its monthly bulletin, the DDKO discussed the economic problems of eastern Turkey, the oppression of Kurdish villagers by Kurdish aghas and sheikhs, and what was termed "the brutal and violent behavior" of the Turkish army units in eastern Turkey.[26]

According to John C. Cooley, demonstrations in eastern Turkey were repeated "on an even larger scale in August 1969, after the killing of two organizers of the Kurdish student organization, the Union of Students" and the DDKO.[27] In the same year, writes Kendal, Turkish "commandos, who had been trained by American specialists in counter-insurgency, launched a vast campaign, raking the Kurdish countryside under the pretext of a general 'arms search.'"[28] This action followed an abortive attempt at joint cooperation with Iraq and Iran termed "Operation Tigris." All of this Kurdish unrest of the 1960s, of course, represented only a relatively small portion of the instability and terrorism that led to the indirect intervention by the Turkish military on March 12, 1971. In restoring order, the new Army-supported government of Prime Minister Nihat Erim soon announced that among numerous other problems "Kurdish nationalism has joined left and right political extremism to threaten Turkey's government."[29] Justice Minister Ismail Arar told Parliament that a "Kurdish movement" aimed at establishing Kurdish independence had stockpiled arms from the eastern bloc countries in cooperation with the Iraqi Kurdish leader, Barzani.[30]

During the next several months, most of the Kurdish activists were included in the thousands of terrorist suspects apprehended by the new government. Kendal wrote that the Diyarbakir military court "sentenced more than a thousand 'Kurdish separatists' between 1971 and 1973."[31] Along with various radical Turkish organizations, the DDKO was banned and security was restored throughout the country by the summer of 1973. Political parties were allowed to resume their activities, and elections were held in the fall of that year.

Once again, Kurdish politicians were able to make use of Turkey's multiparty system by bargaining their important support to the most attractive party. For a while in the 1970s, the new social democratic appeal of Bulent Ecevit's Republican Peoples Party (RPP) looked appealing to many Kurdish leaders. Indeed, before the 1973 elections, Ecevit toured eastern Anatolia promising that he would pay particular attention to the problems of the east. By the 1977 elections, however, most Kurdish leaders had broken with him over an inability to reach a meaningful accommodation.

Even more ominously Turkey began to sink into a crippling spiral of political instability and terrorism as the 1970s drew to a close. This situation, of which the Kurdish problem was only one element, was in turn greatly to influence the course of the Kurdish problem in Turkey. It is to this state of affairs that led to the military intervention headed by General Kenan Evren on September 12, 1980, then, that we must next turn.

### Notes

1. Kendal [Nezan], "The Kurds under the Ottoman Empire," in *People without a Country: The Kurds and Kurdistan*, ed. by Gerard Chaliand (London: Zed Press, 1980), p. 22.

2. *Ibid.*, p. 25.

3. National Foreign Assessment Center (U.S. Central Intelligence Agency), *The Kurdish Problem in Perspective* (Aug. 1979), p. 13. To a British vice-consul, the Sheikh had written in 1878: "The Kurdish nation is a people apart. Their religion is different and their laws and customs are distinct." Cited in Derk Kinnane, *The Kurds and Kurdistan* (London: Oxford University Press, 1964), p. 24.

4. Robert W. Olson, "Four Stages of Kurdish Nationalism: From Sheikh Ubaydallah to Sheikh Said, 1880-1925," paper presented at the 22nd annual meeting of the Middle East Studies Association of North America, Los Angeles, California, Nov. 5, 1988, p. 10.

5. *Ibid.*, p. 13. For a more thorough analysis, see Robert Olson, *The Emergence of Kurdish Nationalism and the Sheikh Said Rebellion, 1880-1925* (Austin: University of Texas Press, 1989).

6. On this point, see Bernard Lewis, *The Emergence of Modern Turkey* (London: Oxford University Press, 1968), pp. 1-5.

7. Ismet Cheriff Vanly, *Le Kurdistan irakien: entite nationale* (Neuchatel: Editions de la Baconniere, 1970), p. 54, as cited in George S. Harris, "Ethnic Conflict and the Kurds," *Annals AAPSS* 433 (Sept. 1977), p. 115.

8. For a detailed analysis of the 1925 rising in addition to the analyses by Olson above, see M.M. van Bruinessen, *Agha, Shaikh and State: On the Social and Political Organization of Kurdistan* (Utrecht, The Netherlands: University of Utrecht, 1978), pp. 353-406. This revolt had both religious and nationalistic overtones. For a shorter analysis of all three revolts from the Kurdish point of view, see Kendal [Nezan], "Kurdistan in Turkey," in *People without a Country: The Kurds and Kurdistan*, ed. by Gerard Chaliand (London: Zed Press, 1980), pp. 61-68.

9. Bruinessen, *Agha, Shaikh and State*, p. 242.

10. Kendal, "Kurdistan in Turkey," p. 68.

11. L. Rambout, *Les Kurdes et le droit* (Paris: Le Cerf, 1947), p. 28. Abdul Rahman Ghassemlou, *Kurdistan and the Kurds* (Prague: Czechoslovak Academy of Sciences, 1965), p. 52; and Edgar O'Ballance, *The Kurdish Revolt: 1961-1970* (Hamden, Conn.: Archon Books, 1973), p. 27, repeated the same figures.

12. David McDowall, *The Kurds*, Report No. 23 (London: Minority Rights Group Ltd., 1985), p. 12.

13. Martin van Bruinessen, "The Kurds in Turkey," *MERIP Reports*, No. 121 (Feb. 1984), p. 8.

14. Kendal, "Kurdistan in Turkey," pp. 68-69.

15. *Kurdish Problem in Perspective*, p. 25.

16. "Memorandum of the Kurdish Rizgari Party, Baghdad, 18th January 1946," in F. David Andrews, ed., *The Lost Peoples of the Middle East: Documents of the Struggle for Survival and Independence of the Kurds, Assyrians, and Other Minority Races in the Middle East* (Salisbury, N.C.: Documentary Publications, 1982), pp. 87-88.

17. See, for example, McDowall, *The Kurds*, p. 13; Bruinessen, "Kurds in Turkey," p. 8; and Kendal, "Kurdistan in Turkey," p. 73. My discussion of the recent background that follows owes a great deal to these sources, particularly Kendal.

18. Bruinessen, "Kurds in Turkey," pp. 8, 12n.1; and "55 Landowners 'Exiled' from Towns," *Christian Science Monitor*, Dec. 5, 1960, p. 14.

19. Kendal, "Kurdistan in Turkey," p. 75.

20. Kinnane, *Kurds and Kurdistan*, pp. 32-33.

21. Cited in *ibid.*, p. 33.

22. Bruinessen, "Kurds in Turkey," p. 8.

23. Cited in Kendal, "Kurdistan in Turkey," p. 97. Also see Ismet Cheriff Vanly, *Survey of the National Question of Turkish Kurdistan with Historical Background* (Zurich: Hevra, [1971]), pp. 51-54.

24. For an analysis of Turkish radicalism at this time see Jacob M. Landau, *Radical Politics in Modern Turkey* (Leiden: E. J. Brill, 1974).

25. The following discussion is largely based on John K. Cooley, "Ankara Admits Kurdish Threat," *Christian Science Monitor*, May 3, 1971, pp. 1, 4. Also see Ismail Besikci, *Dogu Anadolu'nun Duzeni: Sosyo-Ekonomik ve Etnik Temeller* [The Order of Eastern Anatolia: Socio-Economic and Ethnic Foundations] (Istanbul: E. Yayinlari, 1970), pp. 438-50.

26. Bruinessen, "Kurds in Turkey," p. 8.

27. Cooley, "Ankara Admits Kurdish Threat," p. 4.

28. Kendal, "Kurdistan in Turkey," p. 88.

29. Cited in Cooley, "Ankara Admits Kurdish Threat," p. 4.

30. *Ibid.*, p. 1.

31. Kendal, "Kurdistan in Turkey," p. 88.

# 3

# Political Instability and Terrorism in the 1970s

The Republic of Turkey Kemal Ataturk established in the 1920s out of the ruins of the Ottoman Empire was the first new, third-world state of the twentieth century. Modern Turkey antedated the host of other non-European states that began to emerge after World War II by a full generation.

In 1950, Ismet Inonu, Ataturk's successor, decided to end the one-party rule of the Republican Peoples Party (RPP) by allowing Turkey's first genuinely competitive elections. They resulted, however, in his ouster from power. An exaggerated majority election system gave the victorious Democrat Party (DP) of Celal Bayar and Adnan Menderes 86 percent of the National Assembly seats, even though it garnered only 53 percent of the vote. Again in 1954, the election system worked to return Menderes to an even greater, exaggerated majority: 93 percent of the Assembly seats on the basis of 57 percent of the vote.

Thus, when the Turkish military overthrew the increasingly oppressive Menderes regime in 1960 (but then overreacted by unfairly executing him a year later) it allowed the new constitution to alter the electoral system to one of excessive proportional representation (PR) that eventually resulted in a system of rampant multipartyism that hindered and eventually prevented the emergence of any majoritarian government at all.

Even though the military again (this time indirectly) intervened via a "coup by memorandum" in March of 1971 to end a period of terrorism and political instability, it allowed the divisive electoral system of PR to continue when it returned power to the civilians at the end of 1973. Accordingly, throughout most of the 1970s, the political balance of power in the Turkish Parliament was held by two small, right-wing, extremist parties: (1) Necmettin Erbakan's National Salvation Party (NSP), which emphasized Islamic, fundamentalist principles, and (2) Alparslan Turkes's Nationalist Action Party (NAP), which supported a protofascist program of domestic corporatism, pan-Turkic irredentism, and a uniformed youth organization known variously as the *Bozkurt* (Grey Wolves) or the *Ulkucus* (Idealists). This system of stalemated, non-majoritarian, coalitional governments prevailed in the 1970s even though three out of four of Turkey's voters identified with its two main, moderate parties of that era: (1) Suleyman Demirel's center-right Justice Party (JP) and (2) Bulent Ecevit's center-left Republican Peoples Party (RPP).

## Political Deadlock and Extremism

From 1971 to the military coup in 1980, there were ten different governments in Turkey. Not a single one of them represented a majority party in the Grand National Assembly or Turkish Parliament. Indeed only five of them even constituted coalitional majorities formed from the parties represented in the Assembly. The others were either nonpartisan, technocratic cabinets indirectly installed by the military (1971-1974) or minority governments.

During this period, there were two general elections in Turkey. Both were inconclusive since neither one of the two major parties (the RPP and the JP) was able to win a majority.[1] Following the first election, Bulent Ecevit was able to put together a coalitional majority of his left-of-center RPP and Necmettin Erbakan's far-right NSP. This rather cynical, ideological contradiction in terms managed to last long enough to grant what many later would deem an ill-advised general amnesty to thousands of accused terrorists who had been rounded up after the indirect military intervention of 1971.[2] Then, although he successfully managed the intervention in Cyprus during the summer of 1974, Ecevit was forced to resign after failing to consolidate his position in a call for new elections.

After the longest ministerial crisis in modern Turkish history, the first of two so-called national front governments headed by Suleyman Demirel's moderate, right-of-center JP in coalition with the two extremist, right-wing parties of Necmettin Erbakan (NSP) and Alparslan Turkes (NAP) followed. As part of the bargain, both

Erbakan and Turkes were made deputy premiers, with the result that decision-making became all but impossible. One close observer wrote, for example, that "it was not uncommon to hear a policy pronouncement by Premier Demirel flatly contradicted the next day by Deputy Premier . . . Erbakan."[3]

Demirel's first national front coalition lasted from March 1975 until the general election of June 1977 presented Ecevit's opposition RPP with parliamentary seats (213) just short of an absolute majority in the 450-seat Assembly. Ecevit's attempt to parley this result into a successful minority government, however, quickly failed, and Demirel's second national front government returned to power a few weeks later.

Disappointed over his close failure, Ecevit soon was able to entice eleven JP deputies to his side with the promise of ministerial positions, and in January 1978 he entered upon his major governmental opportunity with a great deal of apparent good will. This euphoria soon vanished, however, amid charges of a cynical bargain for power with the eleven JP deputies who had defected, an escalating tide of anarchy and terrorism throughout the country, and a sinking economy that saw crippling shortages of important consumer items, raging inflation, and rising unemployment.

Demirel himself never forgave Ecevit for the manner in which he had come to power and through most of this period even refused to refer to Ecevit by name or as the Prime Minister, an adroit way in which to emphasize how the RPP government was "illegitimate."[4] Near the end of Ecevit's term in office, Demirel blasted him as one "who seized the government with deceit, intrigue and cheating 20 months ago by putting aside the national will."[5] And when he had returned to power in 1980, Demirel on yet another occasion declared concerning Ecevit: "I have doubts about his sanity."[6] For his part Ecevit once described Demirel as: "A party leader who has resorted to the most shameful methods in our political history, who has collaborated with criminals, the person who secured personal benefits from others, the leader of a party which lends deputies to other parties."[7]

The personal invective Turkey's two main political party leaders smeared each other with was more than amply matched by their followers. On a number of occasions "beatings, fights, and foul language" broke out among them in Parliament.[8] Following by-election setbacks in October 1979, Ecevit resigned. Demirel formed a minority government, but the political paralysis only grew.

*Institutional causes.*--Although it is not possible to explain this political deadlock and extremism to everyone's satisfaction, a number of points do seem relevant. First of all, the Turkish political culture had not yet fully been imbued with the concept of the loyal opposition. The 600-year-old authoritarian heritage of the Ottoman Empire had lasted into the twentieth century, and although Kemal Ataturk's political promise had been one of democracy, his own legacy had been that of an authoritarian, one-party regime. The first genuinely competitive elections in Turkey were only held, as noted above, in 1950. When they were, party leaders such as Menderes in the 1950s and Demirel and Ecevit in the 1970s gave too much priority to narrow, short-term party goals, while inhibiting the idea of legitimate opposition.

When in power, each party staked out its own political turf. In time the bureaucracy grew so politicized that even judges, police, university rectors, and other civil servants, as well as mayors and provincial officials, became openly partisan. Thus, although both Ecevit and Demirel began as moderate proponents of western-style democracy, the dynamics of the party system increasingly polarized them and precluded their cooperation. It seems that the mutual hostility of the party leaders and their resulting inability to cooperate for the good of their country might have been the key factor in turning Turkey's multiparty, coalitional-government system of the 1970s on to the road of disaster.[9]

The resulting mudslinging association of the RPP with communism and the JP with fascism began to take on more than just mere appearance. In one egregious example, a partisan of Turkes' NAP headed the customs and monopolies ministry under the Demirel government, even though the NAP was known to have close ties with drug-smuggling activities.[10] Turkes himself was put in charge of internal security and the secret services. As the 1970s progressed, Demirel's JP increasingly became linked with militant Sunni funda-mentalism, as well as rightist trade, teachers, and police unions or associations.

For its part the RPP, given the dearth of other viable left-wing parties, drifted further to the left, co-opting extremists who had nowhere else to go. A number of members of the radical trade union

DISK, for example, were also RPP deputies in the National Assembly. What had started out as the party of Ataturk in the 1920s and, as late as 1972, his chief lieutenant Inonu, had by the late 1970s become, in part, identified with Alevi (Shiite) leftists and Kurdish separatism. Indeed, the electoral prospects of the far left had become so poor that by the mid-1970s Radio Moscow was asking Turkish Marxists to support the RPP.[11] In a post-mortem analysis of what had happened, one of Turkey's leading journalists, Mehmet Ali Birand, observed: "In short, the rules of the game no longer existed in a free for all which dispensed with that principal tenet of democracy, namely, consensus. The people of Turkey looked on as passive spectators at this deadlock in the party political system."[12]

*Sociological causes.*--In addition to the institutional causes analyzed above, a number of sociological factors also contributed to the political deadlock and extremism Turkey experienced in the late 1970s. In his seminal study, Ted Robert Gurr argued:

> The primary causal sequence in political violence is first the development of discontent, second the politicization of that discontent, and finally its actualization in violent actions against political objects and actors. Discontent arising from the perception of relative deprivation is the basic, instigating condition for participants in collective violence.[13]

Building on Gurr's general insights, Paul Magnarella has identified a number of sociological factors which contributed to a sense of relative deprivation and thus helped lead to civil violence and terrorism in Turkey.[14] In the first place, the country's large population (45.4 million by 1980) and rapid urbanization exceeded its available economic opportunities. As Magnarella noted, relative deprivation became "markedly visible in the *gecekondus* (shanty towns) of most cities."[15] The mayor of Istanbul declared "terrorist organizations easily recruit gunmen from among the jobless in the *gecekondus.*"[16] The importation of traditional feuds from the rural areas to the newly created urban areas stimulated more violence.[17]

In addition there were large differences in the distribution of wealth, as well as goods and services, among the Turkish population. High rates of inflation, unemployment, and underemployment compounded the problem. By the end of the 1970s, inflation exceeded 100 percent.[18] Violent incidents resulted directly from this deteriorating economic situation.

What is more the increasing demand for, but limited supply of, higher educational opportunities created additional difficulties. Serif Mardin explained:

> In 1977, 360,000 students competed in the entrance examination to universities for 60,000 places. This leaves 300,000 candidates suspended in mid-stream, with no means of reintegrating them into the employment structure except as disgruntled minor employees with salaries that constitute a pittance by any standards.[19]

Even those who were admitted, however, often found themselves alienated by the overcrowded classrooms and their antiquated memorization methods. Moreover, many who finally did receive a diploma were unable to find employment.

The law on autonomy, which allowed Turkish universities a great deal of immunity from regular police regulation, permitted campuses in the 1970s to become small arsenals and hotbeds of terrorism. Writing in the late 1970s, Serif Mardin noted how old cultural norms reinforced these new legal opportunities: "Student violence, by and large, is directed against other students. The pattern of attack, retaliation, revenge and counter-offensive in which groups are involved is reminiscent of the mechanism of the blood feud in its regularity, symmetry and inevitability."[20] Unwittingly the Turkish system of higher education was also contributing to the growth of the country's political deadlock and extremism.

*Further deadlock.*--This political deadlock and extremism had become so entrenched that when the Turkish military--which saw itself as the ultimate guardian of Turkish democracy[21]--delivered an "opinion" (actually a letter of warning) on December 27, 1979, to "those political parties which could not introduce solutions to the political, economic and social problems . . . that have grown to dimensions threatening the integrity of the country,"[22] it fell upon deaf, paralyzed institutions. Demirel, for example, argued that it could not be meant for his government because it had only been in power for 30 days. Ecevit, on the other hand, determined that since he was now out of office, the warning was not intended for him. "It was as if this opinion [of the military] was directed at a vacuum,"[23] concluded the Turkish military after it finally assumed power nine months later.

The deadlock continued. When President Fahri Koruturk's term ended on April 6, 1980, the paralyzed political parties could not even perform their constitutional duty to elect a new chief of state. As political violence and anarchy (see below) began to take from twenty to thirty lives a day, the Turkish Parliament remained hopelessly deadlocked; more than 100 ballots were taken over a six-month period. Prime Minister Demirel almost seemed to welcome the situation since it enabled a member of his own JP, as presiding officer of the Senate, to act as interim president.

After it toppled this deadlocked regime, the Turkish military declared: "Everyone observed that the political parties had driven into an impasse the election of the highest authority of the State due to calculations of their political interests. . . . The situation was a new example clearly demonstrating the impasse of the Turkish Parliament."[24] Elsewhere too the new military government later declared:

> The political parties, an indispensable element of any democratic society, could not reach a consensus on even the most important issues of state. Their partisan attitudes permeated even the smallest organs in the structure of society. The state institutions, universities, schools (of all levels), security establishments, labour organisations, local administrations, in short, every institution in the country fell under the influence of the political rivalry. These institutions could not function effectively in this atmosphere, and everything got worse.[25]

Even after this deadlocked regime had been toppled and Demirel and Ecevit taken into preventive detention, the two and their respective parties continued their sterile wrangling over the military's proposals for a new, above-politics cabinet. High-ranking officials offered a position by the military first rang up Demirel or Ecevit for advice and approval.[26]

"Jilted by what they saw as the incorrigible mendacity, prevarication and short-sightedness of the political establishment,"[27] the military leaders finally decided to "cut the Gordian knot" by abolishing all the political parties and banning their leaders from any renewed political activity for a period of ten years. Given the impasse they had led their country into, it is difficult to muster much sympathy for these leaders of the old order.

On September 6, 1980, Erbakan staged a massive rally of his NSP followers in the traditionally conservative and religious city of Konya to protest against the Israeli decision to make Jerusalem their capital. Although the military had already decided irrevocably upon intervention, this incident undoubtedly reaffirmed its intention. The description of this event later given by General Evren's new government illustrates graphically the challenge that was being issued to Turkey's secular democracy.

> A big green flag (which symbolizes Islamic law) with Arabic writing was being paraded in front of the crowd. . . . After . . . it was announced that the National Anthem was going to be sung it was observed that a group of the mob sat down on the ground and yelled . . . "we won't sing this march."[28]

## Anarchy and Terrorism

The political deadlock and extremism detailed above inevitably slid into and reinforced outright anarchy and terrorism. A number of leftist terrorist organizations were operating by the late 1970s. They traced their origin from the defunct Turkish Peoples Liberation Party and Front (THKP-C) of Mahir Cayan who, as mentioned in Chapter 2, had been killed in a shootout with Turkish troops in 1972.

Gulten Cayan, Mahir's wife, and a group of sympathizers, however, had managed to escape to Europe following the military crackdown of 1971. There they came to be called the "X-Group." By 1974, they had given way to Dev Genc (Revolutionary Youth), a clearinghouse for leftist revolutionaries of almost every persuasion that had been active since the late 1960s. Splintering in time led to the even more extremist Dev Yol (Revolutionary Way) and Dev Sol (Revolutionary Left) groups, as well as such lesser ones as the THKP-C/Kurtulus or Turkish Peoples Liberation Party and Front/Liberation, the HDO (Revolutionary Pioneers of the People) or Acilciler (Hasty) because of its hasty acceptance of armed action, the MLSPB or Marxist-Leninist Armed Propaganda Unit, and the THKP-C/EB or Turkish Peoples Liberation Party and Front/Action Unit.

Although it is difficult fully to appreciate just how serious this violence became, some indication is offered by the statistical analysis later released by General Evren's new government.[29] The figures that follow graphically illustrate the tremendous buildup of anarchy and terrorism before the military intervention of September 12, 1980, and its speedy demise afterwards.

*Statistical analysis.*--There were a total of 9,795 incidents of clashes and armed attacks during the overall period. Of these, 91 percent occurred before September 12, while only 9 percent took place afterwards. At the same time a total of 6,732 incidents of arson and throwing of explosives took place. Of this figure, 94.5 percent occurred before the military intervention and only 5.5 percent after.

Out of a total of 4,388 incidents of robbery and unlawful acquisition which occurred during the overall period, 68 percent took place during the first period and 32 percent during the second. Furthermore a total of 2,591 student incidents took place at the educational institutions during the time frame examined. Of these, 97.7 percent took place before September 12, while only 2.3 percent occurred afterwards.[30]

During these times, a total of 4,040 people lost their lives as a result of violence, a figure which includes the members of the security forces who were killed, but excludes those from the ranks of the terrorists.[31] Of this total, 92 percent occurred before the military intervention and only 8 percent after. In all, 11,160 people were wounded as a result of terrorist incidents, 93.3 percent before and only 6.7 percent after September 12. Concurrently martial law forces confiscated a total of 804,197 weapons during the overall period. Only 4 percent of these were seized before the military takeover, while the rest were taken after.

Statistical data concerning the political persuasions of the captured terrorists are also useful. In the year following the September 12 intervention, a total of 43,140 persons, including 21,864 leftists, 5,953 rightists, 2,034 (Kurdish) separatists, and 13,289 people whose political orientations have not been established, were arrested.[32] The arrested leftists were responsible for the murder of 729 people and the wounding of 914. The detained rightists had killed 434, while wounding 508. The figures for the apprehended Kurdish separatists were 224 and 251 respectively.

Most of the captured terrorists were males. The monthly income of 89 percent of them was below the TL 10,000 national average of that time, and 79 percent of them were bachelors. In terms of educational levels, the largest group of terrorists (36 percent) had a secondary school education. Those with only an elementary one constituted 28 percent, while illiterates accounted for 22 percent. University school graduates (14 percent) were the smallest group.

The breakdown by profession of the captured terrorists listed (1) students 23 percent, (2) unemployed 20 percent, (3) self-employed 15 percent, (4) workers 14 percent, (5) civil servants 10 percent, (6) teachers 7 percent, and (7) housewives 1 percent. In terms of age the group between 16 and 25 constituted the largest at 57 percent of all the captured terrorists, those between 25 and 35--28 percent, 35 and 45--11 percent, and over 45--4 percent.

Summing up these statistics, General Evren's new government declared: "A careful study of these figures and the causes of the incidents of anarchy and terrorism will clearly show how our youth have been victimized by anarchy and terrorism, the place of workers, teachers, and some civil servants in violence, and the effects of unemployment."[33] Evren's government also blamed certain "foreign states which for years had exploited every opportunity to realize their designs against this country" for this deadly spate of anarchy and terrorism."[34] Indeed some evidence emerged after September 12 to indicate that the Soviet Union and Bulgaria had supplied weapons to the various Turkish terrorist factions, while Syria and the PLO had provided training facilities.[35] The purpose of this foreign intervention was to destabilize a crucial link in the NATO alliance.

On the other hand Mehmet Ali Birand, the respected Turkish journalist who recently wrote a best-seller about the 1980 military coup in Turkey, admitted that with few exceptions "our knowledge today [1987] about the 'wave of terror' of the late 1970s is still as restricted to guess-work and circumstantial evidence as it was at the time."[36] Continuing, he suggested that such sociological factors as Turkey's rapid urbanization and the resulting decline of traditional rural life styles, as well as the "authoritarian personality" in the Turkish culture which made possible "extremist and messianic ideological mobilization,"[38] also played an important role.

*Specific incidents.*--Although the statistics cited above paint an overall picture of the situation, an analysis of some of the specific incidents can give a poignancy to these events that otherwise would be lacking. After it came to power General Evren's government published a lengthy analysis to explain "what sort of conditions prevailed in the country to prompt them [the military] to assume the running of the state. . . . This book sets forth, in an unbiased manner, the real reason for the 12 September operation, by adducing documents and recounting events, in evidence."[39]

One of the first spectacular incidents of anarchy and terrorism occurred on May Day in 1977 when some thirty-seven people were killed at a huge rally organized by the radical trade union DISK in Taksim Square, Istanbul. Although not adequately explained to this day, shots from the surrounding rooftops apparently were fired into the crowd of 200,000 which then panicked and stampeded most of the victims to death.

The report of an incident at Umraniye, Istanbul early in 1978 illustrated how vicious things were becoming.

> The bodies of five workers, apparently murdered after torture, were found in this district. . . . The bodies of the victims . . . were so mutilated as to be almost unidentifiable. Their heads were crushed, eyes gouged out, genitals cut away. The barbarism surpassed belief. These criminals . . . were later to admit cold-bloodedly before the Turkish courts of justice, that they had committed this atrocity as execution of the verdict of their so-called "People's Court."[40]

Shocking as these two events were, both paled before the near civil war of sectarian killing that broke out in the southeastern city of Kahramanmaras in late December 1978. General Evren's government later described what had happened in this manner.

> The country experienced one of its most terrible examples of mass terrorism when a massacre occurred at Kahramanmaras. . . . Security forces prove to be incapable in preventing the incidents. Gendarmery troops from Gaziantep and airborne troops from Kayseri are deployed. . . . Bloodshed goes on. . . . The Council of Ministers proclaims martial law in 13 provinces. . . . A consensus was barely reached. The balance sheet in . . . Kahramanmaras included 109 dead, 176 seriously wounded and 500 houses and shops destroyed.[41]

Five weeks later the single murder of Abdi Ipekci (the distinguished editor of *Milliyet*, one of Turkey's leading newspapers) was eventually to make Turkish terrorism even more notorious in the eyes of international opinion. This was because Ipekci's assassin was

Mehmet Ali Agca. Apprehended several months later, Agca, an apparent member of Turkes's Grey Wolves, escaped from prison with inside help. On May 13, 1981, under circumstances still not entirely clear,[42] Agca came within inches of mortally wounding Pope John Paul II in St. Peter's Square in Rome.

Although these spectacular terrorist attacks made the headlines, Turkey also was increasingly being submitted to a daily drumbeat of more mundane anarchical and terrorist incidents that "were escalating so rapidly that it became impossible to follow who was murdered or wounded and which banks were robbed or which offices were bombed."[43]

The intensity of this anarchy and terrorism continued to escalate in 1980. In January of that year armed clashes between several thousand troops and militant DISK workers at the Taris textile plant in the Aegean port city of Izmir rapidly spread to various other parts of Turkey's third largest city. "Izmir turned into a powder keg. Students also joined the clashes. . . . The workers placed bomb placards in the way of the police and opened fire on fire fighting teams,"[44] stated General Evren's government.

The Tarsus incidents in southeastern Turkey occurred in April and resulted in the death of nine and the wounding of twenty. They were the result of a traffic fatality that leftist elements used to agitate the people into a confrontation with the security forces. "Everything turned into hell at once," the military later explained.[45]

In June right-wing extremists assassinated the District Chairman of the RPP in Nevsehir, a small city some 200 kilometers southeast of Ankara. On June 18, the RPP funeral delegation led by Ecevit travelled to that central Anatolian city, only to be met by a hail of stones and then bullets that wounded five. Abandoning the coffin in the middle of a narrow street, the funeral procession ran for its life. Unable to contact the Prime Minister (Demirel) for help, Ecevit finally was able to get a call through to the Chief of Staff of the Armed Forces (Evren). "General Evren, I can't reach the Prime Minister so I am calling you. My deputies and I have come under gunfire. Our lives are in danger. We are unable to bury our dead. I seek your help and support."[46]

The military responded quickly and order was restored. The supreme irony of the Nevsehir incident, however, was that Ecevit, who as a leftist opposed extraordinary powers for the military, had to call upon it to protect himself and his supporters.

By 1980, 31 of Turkey's 67 provinces reportedly contained so-called "liberated zones," areas under the exclusive authority of one ideological faction or another, and closed off to the state's security forces. One of the most publicized such cases occurred in the remote Black Sea coastal town of Fatsa.[47] Here the radical leftist Dev Yol had set up an alternative regime complete with its own municipal services, "People's Court," and mayor. Only in July of 1980 did the government move against Fatsa, and, as the military later explained, captured "some 300 militants of illegal organizations including the Mayor of the town. . . . An operation carried [out] after 12 September, made clear . . . how this town was turned into [an] experimental site of a regime which was prohibited by our Constitution."[48]

On Friday July 4 a bomb exploded near a mosque in Corum, a city some 200 kilometers east of Ankara, and the area was strafed with bullets. Rumors soon spread that "communists were burning and destroying mosques."[49] Sectarian fighting between Sunni and Alevis broke out "and more than 100 houses and shops were burnt and destroyed on the first day. Nobody could enter the scenes of fire, not even the security forces. . . . Jet fighters carried out deterrent flights over the town."[50] "A correspondent of the national daily newspaper *Milliyet* dispatched to Corum ahead of the armoured brigade barely escaped with his life when he was bundled back into his car and sent packing by right-wing paramilitaries manning road blocks controlling approaches to the city."[51] By the time order was finally restored, at least twenty-three people had been killed.

Less than three weeks later, Dev Sol terrorists gunned down former (1971-1972) Prime Minister Nihat Erim in Istanbul. While his funeral was taking place, Kemal Turkler, the former President of DISK, was assassinated by right-wing terrorists. Bankrupt and paralyzed, the old regime was approaching its inglorious and unlamented end. On September 12 the military mercifully stepped in.

## Conclusions

It is difficult not to admire the military for ending the political deadlock and extremism, as well as the terrible anarchy and terrorism that were threatening the very existence of the Turkish state in the late 1970s. Too many critics of the Evren government fail to appreciate the severity of the situation which existed. Nobody pretends that the military used kid gloves. Few wanted it to. The times called for extraordinary means, and the military proved up to the task. Indeed, given the trying circumstances, one might argue that Evren's government demonstrated relative moderation toward those who had come so close to destroying the state. It is doubtful that a house in such disorder could have been set in order any more lightly than was done after 1980.

What is more there can be no doubt that some of the charges of human rights violations and torture levelled against the regime were politically motivated by the very ones who had tried, but failed, to bring the Turkish state down. "Some of the traitors who fled abroad because of arrests at home following September 12, continued their activities against Turkey in foreign countries and attempted to disseminate through certain international organizations allegations that their supporters in Turkey are being subjected to torture and ill treatment."[52]

Nevertheless the continuing violation of human rights in Turkey today is too well documented to dismiss out of hand.[53] Indeed Evren's government implicitly admitted such abuses. "These elements and other institutions supporting them [those critical of the Evren regime] have never talked about the massacres and torture implemented by the inhuman murderers responsible for thousands of killings and the creation of a climate of fear and intimidation over the Turkish people before September 12."[54] Similarly a well placed Turkish source more recently declared: "That torture, even if not systematic in the sense of being government-controlled, was so wide-spread and a common practice, that only those with political affiliations care about it. The common thief, burglar and what Turks call the 'simple criminal' would just accept it as a way of life."[55]

Teoman Evren, the President of the Union of Turkish Bar Associations, declared in June 1987:

> Not enough action has been taken on torture. Statesmen have not taken definitive actions to end torture, and courts have not followed up torture allegations with sufficient care. The attitude of officials who do not pursue torturers encourages more torture. Statesmen make statements that give heart to torturers, for example, saying that torture takes place all over the world--in Sweden, in the United States.[56]

Both Ecevit and Demirel, who regained their political rights through a special referendum in September 1987, have also spoken out on the matter. Ecevit declared that "torture and arbitrary killings are continuing,"[57] while Demirel added "that 175 or 180 people have died from torture, and that torture is the policy of the current government."[58]

In allowing this situation to continue, the Turkish government is now besmirching the good name of those who saved Turkey from collapse in 1980 and set it successfully upon the road to subsequent democratic and economic renewal. It is encouraging, therefore, that a recent Helsinki Watch report on the situation in Turkey concluded:

> The human rights situation in Turkey remains in a state of flux, but there are still good reasons for optimism. A number of important steps have already been taken by the government to improve the situation and a verbal commitment to human rights and democracy has been publicly made by most of the major political forces in the country. . . . This provides a basis for our continued hope that Turkey will ultimately achieve a government that respects human rights in its actions as well as in its words and provides guarantees for their protection.[59]

### Notes

1. In the 1973 election the RPP won 33.2 percent of the vote, while the JP managed 29.8 percent. The two key right-wing parties, the NSP and NAP, tallied respectively 11.9 percent and 3.4 percent. Two other rightist parties that were more moderate, the Republican Reliance Party (RRP) and the Democratic Party (DP) won 5.3 percent and 11.8 percent of the vote respectively.

In the 1977 election the RPP's hopes for a parliamentary majority fell just short when it managed to win 41.4 percent of the vote, while the JP upped its totals to 36.9 percent. Meanwhile the NSP fell to 8.6 percent, and the NAP rose to 6.4 percent. The other two, more moderate rightist parties, the RRP and DP, were decimated winning respectively just 1.9 percent and 1.8 percent. For a further analysis, see William Hale, "The Role of the Electoral System in Turkish Politics," *International Journal of Middle East Studies* 11 (1980), pp. 401-17.

2. After it came to power in September 1980, for example, the new military government argued: "The comprehensive amnesty proved one of the causes of the new wave of anarchy and terror in the subsequent years."

General Secretariat of the National  Security Council, *12 September in Turkey:  Before and After* (Ankara:  Ongun Kardesler Printing House, 1982), p. 15.  This detailed explanation by the military of the reasons for its intervention will hereafter be cited as *12 September*.  Also see on this point the recent account by the respected Turkish journalist, Mehmet Ali Birand, *The General's Coup in Turkey:  An Inside Story of 12 September 1980*, trans. by M.A. Dikerdem (London:  Brassey's Defence Publishers, 1987) p. 18. Birand's study is based on interviews of 165 of the protagonists of the coup and previously unavailable documents.

    3.    Dankwart A. Rustow, *Turkey:  America's Forgotten Ally* (New York: Council on Foreign Relations, 1987), p. 70.

    4.    On this point see Birand, *General's Coup*, p. 90.

    5.    *12 September*, p. 111.

    6.    *Ibid.*, p. 198.

    7.    *Ibid.*, p. 19.

    8.    See the accounts in *ibid.*, pp. 36, 37, 84, and 93-94.

    9.    On this point, see Ilkay Sunar and Sabri Sayari, "Democracy in Turkey:  Problems and Prospects," in *Transitions from Authoritarian Rule: Prospects for Democracy*, ed. by Guillermo O'Donnell *et al.* (Baltimore and London:  The Johns Hopkins University Press, 1986), p. 182.

    10.  See Rustow, *Turkey*, p. 131n7.

    11.  Lucille W. Pevsner, *Turkey's Political Crisis:  Background, Perspectives, Prospects* (New York:  Praeger, 1984), p. 60.  On the left in general, see George S. Harris, "The Left in Turkey," *Problems of Communism* 29 (July-Aug., 1980), pp. 26-42.

    12.  Birand, *General's Coup*, p. 48.

    13.  Ted Robert Gurr, *Why Men Rebel* (Princeton: Princeton University Press, 1970).  Elsewhere Gurr explained that "relative deprivation . . . [is] defined as actors' perception of discrepancy between their *value expectations* and their environment's apparent value *capabilities*." (Italics in the original.) Ted Robert Gurr, "Psychological Factors in Civil Violence," in *Anger, Violence, and Politics*, ed. by I.K. Feierabend *et al.* (Englewood Cliffs: Prentice Hall, 1972), p. 37.  For analyses of the economic and social changes that occurred in Turkey during the 1970s, see William M. Hale, ed., *Aspects of Modern Turkey* (London:  Bowker, 1976); and Walter Weiker, *The Modernization of Turkey:  From Ataturk to the Present Day* (New York: Holmes & Meier, 1981).

    14.  Paul J. Magnarella, "Civil Violence in Turkey:  Its Infrastructural, Social and Cultural Foundations," in *Sex Roles, Family and Community in Turkey*, ed. by Cigdem Kagitcibasi (Bloomington, Indiana:  Indiana University Turkish Studies, 1982), pp. 383-401.

    15.  *Ibid.*, p. 387.

    16.  Cited in *ibid.*, p. 388.

17. On this point, see Harris, "The Left in Turkey," p. 37.

18. For analyses of Turkey's economic situation in the 1970s, see William M. Hale, *The Political and Economic Development of Modern Turkey* (New York: St. Martin's Press, 1981); and Henri Barkey, "Crises of the Turkish Political Economy of 1960-1980," in *Modern Turkey: Continuity and Change*, ed. by Ahmet O. Evin (Opladen: Leske und Budrich, 1984).

19. Serif Mardin, "Youth and Violence in Turkey," *European Journal of Sociology* 19 (1978), p. 250.

20. *Ibid.*, p. 231.

21. The opening sentence of the military's lengthy explanation for its actions on September 12 speaks about "the Turkish Armed Forces . . . responsibility of 'safeguarding and protecting the Turkish Republic.'" *12 September*, p. ix. For further analyses of the military's unique political role in Turkish politics, see Dankwart A. Rustow, "The Army and the Founding of the Turkish Republic," *World Politics* 11 (July 1959), pp. 513-52; Walter Weiker, *The Turkish Revolution, 1960-1961: Aspects of Military Politics* (Washington: The Brookings Institution, 1963); Ergun Ozbudun, *The Role of the Military in Recent Turkish Politics* (Cambridge, Mass.: Harvard University, Center for International Affairs, 1966): Metin Tamkoc, *The Warrior Diplomats: Guardians of National Security and the Modernization of Turkey* (Salt Lake City: University of Utah Press, 1976); George Harris, *Turkey: Coping with Crisis* (Boulder: Westview Press, 1985), pp. 153-73; and Nicholas S. Ludington and James W. Spain, "Dateline Turkey: The Case for Patience," No. 50 *Foreign Policy* (Spring 1983), pp. 150-68.

22. Cited in *12 September*, p. 160.

23. *Ibid.*, p. 163.

24. *Ibid.*, p. 181.

25. *Ibid.*, p. 27.

26. For the details of this incredible story, see Birand, *Generals' Coup*, pp. 198-208.

27. *Ibid.*, p. 205.

28. *12 September*, pp. 215-16.

29. See the report issued by the Turkish government, *Anarchy and Terrorism in Turkey* [1982]. The following analysis is taken from this source and covers approximately thirty-seven months from December 26, 1978, the date of the proclamation of martial law following the Kahramanmaras incidents (see below), up to February 11, 1982, and is broken down into four separate periods: (1) December 26, 1978-September 11, 1979; (2) September 12, 1979-September 11, 1980; (3) September 12, 1980-September 11, 1981; and (4) September 12, 1981-February 11, 1982. It should be noted that the first two periods took place during the rampant build up of anarchy and terrorism before the military takeover, while the third and fourth periods followed that event. To simplify the process of comparison, these four time

periods will be collapsed into two: before the military intervention and after.

30. I have related some of my experiences as a Senior Fulbright Lecturer at the Middle East Technical University in Ankara during these troubled times (September 1978-June 1979) in Michael M. Gunter, "On Turkish Students," in *The Fulbright Experience, 1946-1986*, ed. by Arthur P. Dudden and Russell R. Dynes (New Brunswick, New Jersey: Transaction Books, 1987), pp. 281-84.

31. A total of 230 members of the security forces were killed, 164 before and 66 after the military intervention. At the same time 348 terrorists died, 146 before and 202 after September 12.

32. Some of these people were released after investigations established their innocence.

33. *Anarchy and Terrorism in Turkey*, p. 14.

34. See *12 September*, p. 6.

35. On this general point also see Paul B. Henze, "Organized Crime and Drug Linkages," in *Hydra of Carnage: International Linkages of Terrorism, The Witnesses Speak*, ed. by Uri Ra'anan *et al.* (Lexington, Mass.: D.C. Heath and Company, 1986), pp. 171-87; and the testimony given by Aydin Yalcin in "Hearing Before the Subcommittee on Security and Terrorism of the Committee on the Judiciary United States Senate on Turkish Experience with Terrorism" (Serial No. J-97-43), 97th Cong., 1st sess., 1981. For a further analysis, see Chapter 7 below.

36. Birand, *Generals' Coup*, p. 51.

37. *Ibid.*, p. 49.

38. *Ibid.*, pp. 51-52.

39. *12 September*, preface.

40. *Ibid.*, pp. 43-44.

41. *Ibid.*, pp. 56-58.

42. On the possible Soviet involvement here, see Claire Sterling, *The Time of the Assassins: Anatomy of an Investigation* (New York: Holt, Rinehart and Winston, 1983); and Paul B. Henze, *The Plot to Kill the Pope* (New York: Charles Scribner's Sons, 1985). For a conflicting opinion see Edward S. Herman and Frank Brodhead, *The Rise and Fall of the Bulgarian Connection* (New York: Sheridan Square Publications, Inc., 1986). Stephen E. Tabachnick has written an insightful review of all three of these analyses. See "Dedefining Reality," *American Book Review*, Jan./Feb. 1987, pp. 9-10. For the most thorough analysis, however, see Jeffrey M. Bale, "The Ultranationalist Right in Turkey and the Attempted Assassination of Pope John Paul II," unpublished manuscript, University of California, Berkeley, Apr. 12, 1989.

43. *12 September*, p. 143.

44. *Ibid.*, p. 170.

45. *Ibid.*, p. 182.

46. Cited in Birand, *Generals' Coup*, p. 143.

47. For a balanced account of Fatsa, see Barry Newman, "The Left, the Right and Hazelnuts: The Nightmare of a Turkish Town," *The Wall Street Journal*, Apr. 29, 1983, p. 1.

48. *12 September*, p. 199.

49. *Ibid.*, p. 194.

50. *Ibid.*

51. Birand, *Generals' Coup*, p. 147.

52. *Anarchy and Terrorism in Turkey*, p. 19.

53. Amnesty International, *Continuing Violations of Human Rights in Turkey* (London: Amnesty International Publications, 1987); and Helsinki Watch Committee, *State of Flux: Human Rights in Turkey* (New York and Washington: U.S. Helsinki Watch Committee, 1987), hereafter cited as *Human Rights in Turkey*. In addition see the other publications of the Helsinki Watch Committee entitled *Violations of the Helsinki Accords: Turkey* (New York and Washington: U.S. Helsinki Watch Committee, 1986); *Freedom and Fear: Human Rights in Turkey* (New York and Washington: U.S. Helsinki Watch Committee, 1986); *Straws in the Wind: Prospects for Human Rights and Democracy in Turkey* (New York and Washington: U.S. Helsinki Watch Committee, 1984); and *Human Rights in Turkey's 'Transition to Democracy'* (New York and Washington: U.S. Helsinki Watch Committee, 1983). Also see the various annual reports by Amnesty International and that organization's *Torture in the Eighties* (London: Amnesty International Publications, 1984).

54. *Anarchy and Terrorism*, p. 19.

55. *Briefing* (Ankara), Feb. 15, 1988, p. 14.

56. *Human Rights in Turkey*, p. 52.

57. *Ibid.*, p. 59.

58. *Ibid.*

59. *Ibid.*, p. 7.

# 4

---

# Suppression

As indicated above in Chapter 2, the official ideology of the Republic of Turkey since the mid-1920s has sought to deny the existence of the Kurdish people in that country. To do this, the authorities attempted to eliminate much that might suggest a separate Kurdish nation. A broad battery of devices was employed to achieve this aim. In some cases what can only be termed pseudo-theoretical justifications were offered do defend what was being done. Thus, both Turks and Kurds were taught that they were descended from the pure Turkish race. Isolated in the mountain fastnesses of eastern Anatolia, the Kurds had simply forgotten their mother tongue. The much abused and criticized appellation "mountain Turks" when referring to the Turkish Kurds served as a code term for these actions. The obvious purpose was to make the Turkish Kurds not only politically Turks (as legally they already were), but also culturally and socially Turks through assimilation.

A ban on the Kurdish language was one major method employed. According to Kendal [Nezan]--a Turkish Kurdish physicist who fled from Turkey in 1971 and has since become a major critic of the Turkish government's policies in his role as the Director of the Kurdish Institute in Paris--this led to a situation where "the authorities banned even the spoken use of Kurdish, at a time when only a tiny minority (3 to 4%) of Kurds spoke any Turkish at all."[1] Even today, again according to Kendal, "despite all efforts, most of them coercive, more than three-quarters of the Kurds in Turkey still do not speak the official language of the state."[2] An "Appeal" by the Socialist Party of Turkish Kurdistan (SPTK) declares that "up until now our people in Turkish . . . Kurdistan have neither been able nor permitted to receive instruction and education in our own language, either publicly or privately. There are no schools either in Turkey or Iran in which the Kurdish language is taught."[3]

Again to cite Kendal: "In Turkey there are colleges and universities where the teaching is in French or in German or in English--but there is not one school where teaching is carried out in Kurdish, the language spoken by about one-quarter of the population."[4] As for publishing, "newspapers, books and records are available in half a dozen non-Turkish languages, but the Kurdish people still cannot publish in their own tongue."[5]

The SPTK tells the following story about its attempt to publish a Kurdish-Turkish journal, *Roja Welat*, in the relatively open society of the mid-1970s. "When our friends applied for permission they were told by the police 'you cannot publish a Kurdish paper. If you do, we will cut your heads off. . . . You can publish in English, French or even in Bengali or Vietnamese if you like. But not in Kurdish.'"[6] When the journal was published in spite of this warning, its chief editor and the owner were arrested and sentenced to one and one-half years' imprisonment. After the military takeover in September 1980, the owner, Mustafa Aydin, was sentenced to "12 years of hard prison confinement. He is still in prison today."[7]

The SPTK also asserts that: "It is forbidden to listen to the Kurdish programmes of foreign broadcasts. It is even forbidden on private occasions, e. g. at parties and marriages, to sing in Kurdish; the sale of [Kurdish] cassettes and records is prohibited." Furthermore, claims the SPTK, although the traditional Kurdish costume was formally banned in 1924, it was unofficially allowed to reappear in the 1970s. After the 1980 military takeover, however, its restriction has been enforced again.

Since 1982, declares the SPTK, "government officials received instructions to register only 'respectable' Turkish names. . . . In particular, those names ending with 'o', a typical Kurdish name form, are no longer permitted. Families giving their children Kurdish names are persecuted."[8] The U.S Helsinki Watch Committee, a group founded in 1979 to promote domestic and international compliance with the human rights provisions of the 1975 Helsinki accords, recently verified this situation regarding Kurdish names. A Turkish legal document translated by the Committee indicated that on May 6, 1983, the Turkish District Court in the eastern province of Agri, found that "the first names of Ali Ekrem Kutley's children do not correspond to the record regulations as stated in Article 77." The court went on to declare:

> The names Brusk and Bineos are contradictory to good morals, damage the national culture and tradition, and affect the interests of the Turkish Republic. Therefore . . . the names should be emended. . . . The children of the accused . . . will be called Mehmet and Emine. . . . Appeals will not be allowed.[9]

The SPTK has further charged that "the government destroyed . . . the inscriptions on the city walls of Diyarbakir because they told about Kurds. . . . The Turkish government . . . even changed the names of the villages, provinces, mountains and rivers of Kurdistan."[10]

Over the years a number of Turkish Kurds have been forced to move to parts of western Turkey. Recently new population transfers have begun again, ostensibly to provide better services or protect the villagers from guerrilla attacks. The SPTK, however, argues "that this deportation plan is part of the continuing attempts since 1923 by successive Turkish regimes to destroy the Kurdish identity."[11] Even the massive GAP Plan to develop southeastern Turkey by damming the Euphrates River has been criticized for similar reasons: "It is the ancient culture of the 8 million to 10 million indigenous Kurds that will be drowned by the dam . . . [to further] the decades-old policy to annihilate the Kurdish presence in Turkey."[12]

As noted above in Chapter 2, the present (1982) Turkish constitution sanctions this suppression of the Kurdish language and culture in several ways. Article 26 states: "No language prohibited by law shall be used in the expression and dissemination of thought. Any written or printed documents, phonograph records, magnetic or video tapes, and other media instruments used in contravention of this provision shall be confiscated." Article 28 declares: "Publications shall not be made in any language prohibited by law."

Other constitutional devices that have been employed include: Article 57 which stipulates that all political activity must promote "the indivisibility of the national homeland"; and Article 89 which provides, in part, that "no political party may concern itself with the defense, development, or diffusion of any non-Turkish language or culture; nor may they seek to create minorities within our frontiers or to destroy our national unity." In addition, the Turkish Penal Code has been used to stifle manifestations of Kurdish nationalism. Articles 141 and

142, for example, prohibit forming organizations or making propaganda aimed at establishing the "domination of a social class over other social classes."

Since 1980, thousands of suspected Kurdish separatists have been arrested by the Turkish government. David McDowall asserts that "in Turkey the Kurds feature prominently amongst those receiving the harshest treatment from the government."[13] The internationally respected Amnesty International (AI) organization concluded that "torture was widespread and systematic and that most people detained by police and martial law authorities were subjected to torture, which in some cases was alleged to have ended in death."[14]

In another report, AI expressed its "concern about the deteriorating state of health of many prisoners in Diyarbakir Military Prison. This was due to torture, harsh prison conditions and insufficient medical attention. Particularly mentioned were Mehdi Zana, Pasa Uzun, Mumtaz Kotan and Huseyin Yildirim. . . . Similar information was received from Serafettin Kaya."[15] All of these individuals were prominent Turkish Kurds "charged with separatist activities and who were not accused of involvement in violence."[16] Indeed, Zana, who was sentenced to thirty-two years in prison, was the former mayor of Diyarbakir itself.

According to Kurdish sources, in 1968, Emin Bozarslan published an ABC primer for Kurdish children in Turkey. The Turkish courts banned the book two days later leading to a situation in which "the only forbidden spelling book on earth is Kurdish."[17] More recently, the Turkish Embassy in Copenhagen, Denmark protested when Bozarslan tried to open a course for teachers in the Kurdish language there.[18]

In March 1981, Serafettin Elci, who served as Minister of Public Works under Prime Minister Bulent Ecevit in the late 1970s, was sentenced to two years and three months in prison for "making Kurdish and secessionist propaganda."[19] The former minister, who is Kurdish, apparently was convicted on the basis of published statements in which he stated: "I am a Kurd. There are Kurds in Turkey."

In March 1973, Franz Reissig, the deputy manager of the Istanbul office of Lufthansa, supposedly was jailed because he had inadvertently photographed an antique globe which bore the names "Armenia," "Pontus," and "Kurdistan" for an airline advertisement.[20] Two doctors, who were members of the French medical team Medicin du Monde, allegedly were imprisoned for more than five months because they possessed a Kurdish music tape and a pamphlet on the Kurds in French.[21] In May 1984, a Turkish subscriber to the *Oriental Rug Review*, an American publication on carpets, supposedly was arrested because he carried a recent issue that featured Kurdish rugs.[22] The internationally renowned film maker Yilmaz Guney, a Turkish Kurd, was banned in his own country.[23]

### Ismail Besikci

Possibly the *cause celebre* of the cases dealing with the suppression of the Turkish Kurds involves a Turkish sociologist who is not even Kurdish, Dr. Ismail Besikci. This academic spent more than ten years in prison for his writings on the Turkish Kurds in which he documented what he claimed were injustices committed against them and showed that they constituted a nation with a distinct language, culture, and heritage worthy of protection from enforced assimilation.

Born in Corum, Turkey in 1939, Besikci first met some Kurds when he was a student at Ankara University's Faculty of Political Science.[24] Afterwards he did his graduate research and military service in eastern Turkey. Based on these lengthy experiences, he wrote his doctoral dissertation which was published in 1969 as *Dogu Anadolu'nun Duzeni: Sosyo-Ekonomik ve Etnik Temeller* (The Order of Eastern Anatolia: Socio-Economic and Ethnic Foundations). Although no qualified academic has attempted to refute or make a serious critique of his findings or research methodology, Besikci was stripped of his academic titles, dismissed from his position at Ataturk University in Erzurum, accused of being an "agent" working in collaboration with unspecified "internal and external agents" bent on dividing Turkey and the Turkish nation, and sentenced to prison for making "Communist and Kurdish propaganda."

His first incarceration occurred in 1971 after the indirect military coup in that year. Released in 1974 following Ecevit's general amnesty, Besikci wrote three more studies on Kurdish sociology and history which led to a new prison term in 1979-1981. Rearrested only two months after his release for writing a thank-you letter to Madame Mousse Boulanger, the Chairperson of the Swiss Union of Writers, Besikci remained imprisoned until May 25, 1987, for publishing "in a foreign country baseless and false information about the internal affairs of Turkey in such a way as to diminish the influence and prestige of the state." He was detained again by the police on

December 29, 1988, for an interview he gave to the monthly, *Ozgur Gelecek.*

In his letter to Madame Boulanger, dated August 14, 1980, Besikci, in part, asserted:

> The official ideology in Turkey continues to maintain in an insistent and obstinate manner that there are no people known as Kurds and no language known as Kurdish. . . . University circles, political parties, unions, associations, mass media etc. never touch on the Kurdish question. The aim is to dismiss those who have an interest in the question of Kurdistan. . . . And today, Kurdistan in the centre of the Middle East is an international colony that has been divided and severed and whose . . . national and democratic rights have been confiscated. The Kurdish people are a nation partitioned by barbed-wires and fields of mines with on-going efforts to completely cut off the parts from one another. Under these conditions, the political status of the Kurdish people is even lower than that of a colony. Because, for example, in Turkey even their existence is not accepted. The Kurds in Turkey can have rights only to the extent of becoming Turks. The alternative is repression, cruelty, prison. . . .[25]

In an article written in October 1987, Besikci renewed his critique of the Turkish state's suppression of its Kurds:

> It has been asserted in Turkey that Kurds are really Turks, and that a Kurdish nation or a Kurdish language do not exist. This view is propagated by all the means at the disposal of the state, from the universities to the repressive apparatus. Any opposition to this view is considered subversive and is immediately punished. Official ideology thus presents itself as the greatest obstacle to scientific inquiry. . . . Court decisions 'prove' that Kurds do not exist and Kurds are imprisoned for laying claim to reality. In such a situation it is impossible for a scientist to claim objectivity since it becomes impossible to engage in the unrestrained criticism which characterizes scientific discourse. . . . There is only one way to avoid this distortion: to reject the ban imposed by state ideology and declare it incompatible with a scientific approach.[26]

Still undaunted, Besikci told a Western news source in August 1989 that the current Kurdish violence "is partly a reaction to repression."[27] Warming to his task, he added that "for decades state policy against the Kurds has been one of terror and repression." Early in 1990, Besikci was reportedly arrested once again.

Despite these opinions, Besikci's supporters claim that he has never advocated or resorted to violence for any purpose and that he has not been associated with any group advocating or resorting to violence. He always has carried on his research, analyzed his data, and published his findings it is asserted, in a scholarly and professional matter. He also has invited fellow sociologists, historians, political scientists, and other interested parties to review, criticize, and comment on his work.

Nevertheless, in addition to his lengthy prison sentences, Besikci stated to Helsinki Watch in June 1987 that while he was incarcerated he underwent torture on a number of occasions. Based on these facts, Amnesty International adopted Besikci as a "prisoner of conscience."

## Recent Events

Although Turkey currently has a vigorous press that spans the political spectrum and the heretofore forbidden word "Kurd" can now be printed, major problems concerning freedom of the press still exist. Many involve the Kurdish problem. In June 1988, for example, Mehmet Ali Birand, one of the country's leading journalists, began publication of his interview with Abdullah (Apo) Ocalan, the leader of the Kurdish guerrilla group in southeastern Turkey called the Kurdish Workers Party (PKK). The interview ran for two days in *Milliyet,* one of the country's leading newspapers, but further publication was then halted by the government. One month later charges were brought against Birand and Eren Guvener, the "responsible editor" or one legally liable for anything illegal the paper printed. The two were charged with publishing "propaganda detrimental to feelings of patriotism in Turkey," in violation of Article 142 of the Penal Code. Both faced 15-year prison sentences until finally acquitted in 1989. Nevertheless the pressure exerted by the government will undoubtedly cause others to think twice before publishing things about the Kurds.

A recent, scholarly analysis published in Britain by Aydin Zulkuf is a case in point.[28] Although this study purported to be on "Underdevelopment and Rural Structures in Southeastern Turkey" (and in some ways is a credible work) it incredibly does not once make a single mention of the word "Kurd." One who did not know otherwise could read the entire book without knowing whom the author was supposedly studying. It is as if one were analyzing a population without examining the people.

Several leftist political journals, chief among which is *2000'e Dogru* (Toward 2000), have run into even more problems in publishing material on the Kurdish problem. As of March 1989, the responsible editor of the journal, Fatma Yazici, was preparing to serve a prison sentence of eight and one half years. Thirteen of the twenty-eight charges against *2000'e Dogru* involved the Kurdish issue.

(1) In March 1989, an appeals court upheld a sentence of more than six years for Yazici because her journal had published a summary of a Helsinki Watch report on the Kurdish problem in Turkey the previous year. She had been found guilty of "weakening national sentiments."[29]   (2) A three-year sentence was handed down for "making anti-Turkish propaganda" in the issue of March 27, 1988. The problem involved publishing a paid obituary which marked the second anniversary of the death of the Kurdish guerrilla leader, Mahsun Korkmaz, during a fight with government forces.

(3) On July 3, 1988, *2,000'e Dogru* published an appeal by a number of well-known people from around the world calling for the protection of the Kurdish culture in Turkey. The journal was indicted for "weakening national sentiments."   (4) An indictment for similar reasons was made when a letter of the famous Turkish communist poet Nazim Hikmet (who died in 1963) on Turkish-Kurdish brotherhood was published in the issue of July 31, 1988.   (5) An earlier issue from 1987 was confiscated before it could even be distributed because it contained the minutes of Ataturk's press conference in 1923 on "Autonomy for Kurds."   In late June of 1989, the journal was again banned by the Istanbul State Security Court for making comparisons between the suppression of the Turkish Kurds and the Bulgarian Turks.[30]

Several other Turkish authors and journalists also suffered legal problems recently because of what they published concerning the Kurdish problem in their country.   On March 10, 1988, Cengiz Turhan, the editor-in-chief of *Yeni Gundem* (New Agenda), was sentenced to seven and one half years in prison for publishing an interview with Kendal Nezan, the Director of the Kurdish Institute in Paris.[31]   In January 1989, the owner and general manager of *Ozgur Gelecek* was charged with "making separatist propaganda" when he republished the letter written by Nazim Hikmet on Turkish-Kurdish brotherhood which appeared earlier in *2,000'e Dogru*.[32]   Professor

Server Tanilli also was accused in January 1988, of "making separatist propaganda" in his book *What Kind of Democracy Do We Want?*

Musicians too have come under fire when they touched on the sensitive Kurdish issue in Turkey. Efkan Sesen and Tuncay Akdogan, members of the folk music group *Yorum* (Commentary), were detained in Ankara in November 1988 for singing Kurdish songs.[33] Ibrahim Tatlises, a popular folk singer, was asked at a cultural evening in Usak, Turkey to sing in Kurdish. He declined by declaring: "I am a Kurd, but the laws ban me from singing in Kurdish." He was prosecuted for "separatist propaganda."[34]

On February 8, 1989, the disciplinary council of the Social Democrat Populist Party (SHP) suspended Ibrahim Aksoy, the parliamentary deputy from Malatya, for two years because of comments he made about the Kurdish problem the previous month in Strasbourg at the mixed Turco-European parliamentary commission. Aksoy, who is of Kurdish descent, had spoken about the need "to give cultural autonomy to the Kurds, who are not a minority, but a nation."[35]

Although his parliamentary immunity protected Aksoy from any further sanctions, Prime Minister Turgut Ozal made political capital out of the situation: "With such ideas, the SHP could never govern the country; it would only cut it to pieces."[36] Mukerrem Tascioglu, the deputy chairman of Ozal's party, added: "Some Turks speak dialects but there is no Kurdish minority in Turkey."[37]

Reports that some of the inhabitants of the southeastern Anatolian village of Yesilyurt were forced to eat human excrement by a Turkish army unit in January 1989 caused much unfavorable opinion in Turkey. A parliamentary member of Ozal's governing Motherland Party (ANAP) declared: "We are asking for an explanation. The state cannot act like a bandit in the Yesilyurt affair."[38]

*Eren comments.*--On January 19, 1988, Mehmet Ali Eren, a member of the Turkish parliament from the opposition SHP and of Kurdish ancestry, caused an uproar when he explicitly broached the Kurdish problem. It was maybe the first time such a speech had been made in that body.[39]

Eren pointed out that "the existence of the Kurds has been continually denied. These citizens have always been looked on with suspicion. . . . In the East the entire population . . . is held responsible for the most minor incident and the peasants are submitted to all kinds of bad treatment." Flaunting the official national ideology of his country, Eren proclaimed: "The Kurds constitute a national minority," and then elaborated: "They [the Turkish Kurds] cannot speak or write freely in their language. They cannot give their children the names of their choice." Concluding that "today one of the social blights which preoccupies permanently public opinion is the Kurdish question," the SHP deputy recommended: "The Kurdish question should be broached in all its dimensions; we should find realistic solutions for it and the question should be debated."

Eren's speech evoked loud boos from the governing ANAP members of parliament. At one point, some of them even began to beat their desks in a sign of protest. The following citations indicate some of the responses made by them. Halim Aras (Koaceli): "You lie. . . . What a lie." Ilhan Askin (Bursa): "You don't know what you're talking about." Seref Bozkurt (Ankara): "You use words which attack our national unity. . . . This deputy is guilty of a crime against the Constitution. . . . There is no Kurdish element; there is only the Turkish nation." Oltan Sungurlu (Minister of Justice): "Mr. President, words contrary to the Constitution have been pronounced here. Who is then this minority in Turkey; let him say it; don't let him speak in this fashion."

Former Prime Minister and present head of the True Path Party (DYP) in parliament, Suleyman Demirel, denounced Eren's speech as a "knife stab at the indivisible unity of the Turkish nation." Kosksal Toptan, the vice president of Demirel's party, declared: "The right to speak freely does not mean the right to destroy the state and the regime." Illustrating the magnitude of the taboo on things Kurdish broached by Eren, Toptan added: "The fact that an honorable deputy could, in the national assembly chamber, speak of the existence in Turkey of a minority nation goes beyond comprehension."

Erdal Inonu, the leader of the SHP opposition, however, simply criticized Eren for having "expressed his opinions poorly," adding that "the word 'minority' that he used in his speech has been misunderstood and provoked the incidents. . . . I myself noted that his terms are erroneous." Somewhat incongruously, Inonu then declared: "there is nothing in what he said which would be contrary to the principles of our party." Early in February, the Turkish parliament decided to apply little-used Article 83 of the Turkish constitution under which Eren's speech would not be allowed to be repeated outside of that body. Although he enjoyed parliamentary immunity, given the uproar he had caused, Eren got off with a very light rebuke.

## Turkish Rationale

Adnan Kahveci, a special adviser to Prime Minister Ozal, recently explained the Turkish rationale for pursuing the policy it does concerning the Kurds.[40] After noting the ethnic diversity of modern Turkey ("Many people, speaking different languages and dialects, came to Anatolia in a mass exchange of immigrants . . . to set up a single nation."), Kahveci acknowledged that "a Turk ethnically may be a Laz, Kurd, Circassian, Bochnak, Albanian, etc." He argued, however, that "the founders of the Republic, namely M. Kemal Ataturk and the Parliament, thought that only a single language could create a strong society with no ethnic discrimination."

Kahveci maintained that the "one language, unified culture approach" had led to the situation where "in Turkey, there is no difference between a Turk or a Kurd. A Turk is defined as a person who is a citizen of this country." Pointing out how a number of Republican Turkey's leaders "were born in eastern Turkey," Kahveci proudly declared that "nobody even questioned them about whether they had [a] Kurdish background. . . . The notion of ethnic discrimination does not exist in this society."[41] Therefore, he argued, "when a European asks the question 'Why are there no Kurdish language schools?', it has no pertinence to the Turkish social structure."

In conclusion, Kahveci declared that "if the founders of the Republic had decided that each ethnic group could have its own language . . . Turkey would today be like Lebanon. Different languages would have stimulated ethnic problems." As Mukerrem Tascioglu, the head of the Turkish parliamentary delegation to Strasbourg, noted a year later: "If we open the door with Kurdish, there will next be Tartar and Laz and Turkey will become a 70-piece patchwork. We cannot sacrifice our national unity."[42]

Discussing the Turkish Kurdish film maker Yilmaz Guney, and the notion that "any movie that advocates two different races harms the national unity," however, Kahveci hinted at the possibility of change in the future: "Ten years from now, maybe it won't be so controversial. . . . You can see that we nearly had a civil war here in 1980. . . . To eradicate those prejudices takes a lot of time. . . . Maybe it will all change in a couple of years."[43] Prime Minister Ozal recently stated that "it was not an offence to speak the Kurdish language in private,"[44] and prisoners are now permitted to converse with visitors in Kurdish if they so choose. Despite these halting steps, the Turkish suppression of the Kurdish language and culture remains a glaring inconsistency upon that government's democratic record.

## Notes

1. Kendal [Nezan], "Kurdistan in Turkey," in *People without a Country: The Kurds and Kurdistan*, ed. by Gerard Chaliand (London: Zed Press, 1980), p. 83.
2. *Ibid.*, p. 84. Kendal cites figures from the Turkish newspaper *Cumhuriyet* (31 July 1966) to state that "in Mardin, 91% of the population speak not a word of Turkish; in Siirt, the figure is 87%; in Hakkari 81%; in Diyarbekir 67%; in Bingol 68%; in Bitlis 66%; etc." These figures seem exaggerated. Virtually all males in Turkey, for example, must serve in the military where they have to speak Turkish. Thus, it would seem, at least 50 percent of the Turkish Kurds must speak some Turkish.
3. Socialist Party of Turkish Kurdistan (SPTK), "Appeal to the Delegates of the 23rd General Conference of the UNESCO, Sofia/Bulgaria," 8 October, 1985.
4. Kendal, "Kurdistan in Turkey," p. 85.
5. *Ibid.*
6. Socialist Party of Turkish Kurdistan (SPTK), "A Report of the Address by Kemal Burkay, General Secretary of the Socialist Party of Turkey Kurdistan, to the Labour Movement Conference on Turkey Held 22nd September, 1984, at the Headquarters of the NUR," n. d.
7. SPTK, "Appeal to UNESCO." This citation and the following data were taken from this document.
8. *Ibid.*
9. U.S. Helsinki Watch Committee, *Destroying Ethnic Identity: The Kurds of Turkey* (New York and Washington: U.S. Helsinki Watch Committee, 1988), pp. 67-69.
10. SPTK, "Appeal to UNESCO."
11. SPTK, "Report on the Violation of Human Rights in Turkish-Kurdistan," No. 3, April 1987. Similarly, the U.S. Helsinki Watch Committee reported that "the local [Kurdish] leaders with whom we spoke believed that the real purpose [of the population transfer] was to assimilate the Kurds--to end their separate cultural existence." U.S. Helsinki Watch Committee, *Destroying Ethnic Identity*, pp. 37-38. Also see "Minorities in the Gulf War," *Cultural Survival Quarterly* 11 (No. 4, 1987), p. 29.

12. Vera Beaudin Saeedpour, "Ataturk and the Kurds," (letter to the editor) *Engineering News-Record*, Sept. 18, 1986.

13. David McDowall, *The Kurds*, Report No. 23 (London: Minority Rights Group Ltd., 1985), p. 27.

14. Amnesty International, *Torture in the Eighties* (London: Amnesty International Publications, 1984), p. 217.

15. Amnesty International, *Amnesty International Report 1983* (London: Amnesty International Publications, 1983), p. 282.

16. *Ibid.*, p. 281. Also see "The Torture of Huseyin Yildirim," *MERIP Reports*, No. 121 (Feb. 1984), pp. 13-14. On the other hand, as discussed below in Chapter 6, Yildirim became the European spokesman for the PKK, the Turkish Kurdish party currently carrying out a guerrilla war in southeastern Turkey.

17. Vera Beaudin Saeedpour (The Kurdish Program Cultural Survival, Inc.), "The Kurdish Way of Life in Turkey: A Tapestry of Tribulations," *Kurdish Times* 1 (Spring 1986), p. 9.

18. U.S. Helsinki Watch Committee, *Destroying Ethnic Identity*, p. 10.

19. This and the following information were taken from Marvine Howe, "Turks Imprison Former Minister Who Spoke Up on Kurds' Behalf," *New York Times*, Mar. 27, 1981.

20. Saeedpour, "Kurdish Life in Turkey," p. 9.

21. *Ibid.*

22. *Ibid.*

23. Few know, however, that Guney murdered a Turkish judge in 1974 during a brawl in a restaurant. He died in exile in Paris in September 1984. In general, see "Temoin du peuple turc: La mort de Yilmaz Guney," *Le Monde*, Sept. 11, 1984.

24. The following analysis is largely based on "The Trial of Ismail Besikci," *Kurdish Times* 2 (Fall 1986), pp. 3-44; data supplied by Michael Maher, a member of the Australian Parliament, and dated January 22, 1985; Lale Yalcin, "Ismail Besikci: State Ideology and the Kurds," *Middle East Report*, No. 153 (July-August, 1988), p. 43; and the U.S. Helsinki Watch Committee, *Destroying Ethnic Identity*, pp. 9-10.

25. This translation of Besikci's letter was supplied by Michael Maher, a member of the Australian Parliament.

26. This translation of Besikci's article was made in Yalcin, "Ismail Besikci," p. 43.

27. This and the following citation were taken from Aliza Marcus, "Battle for Control of a Province," *Christian Science Monitor*, Aug. 25, 1989, p. 6.

28. Aydin Zulkuf, *Underdevelopment and Rural Structures in Southeastern Turkey: Gisgis and Kalhana* (London: Ithaca Press, 1986). In truth there actually is one time the word "Kurd" appears in this book, not in the text,

but buried at the end in a lengthy bibliography that cites one of the works of Ismail Besikci, who used the word in his title.

29. This and the following data were taken from U.S. Helsinki Watch Committee, *Paying the Price: Freedom of Expression in Turkey* ([New York and Washington]: U.S. Helsinki Watch Committee, 1989), pp. 31-34. See also Lois Whitman and Thomas Fromeck, "In Turkey, Being a 'Responsible Editor' Often Means Prison," *International Herald Tribune*, Feb. 25, 1989.

30. "2,000'e Dogru Banned," *Turkey Briefing* (Britain), July 1989.

31. "Turquie: un journaliste condamne," *Tribune De L'Expansion*, Mar. 10, 1988.

32. U.S. Helsinki Watch Committee, *Paying the Price*, p. 53.

33. *Ibid.*, p. 102.

34. *Ibid.*, pp. 102-103.

35. Cited in Institut Kurde de Paris, *Information and Liaison Bulletin* (Paris), No. 46-47-48 (Jan.-Feb.-Mar., 1989), pp. 7-8.

36. *Ibid.*, p. 8.

37. Cited in "When is a Kurd not a Kurd," *Briefing* (Ankara), Feb. 13, 1989, p. 9.

38. Cited in *Cumhuriyet*, Jan. 31, 1989.

39. The following citations were taken from Institut Kurde de Paris, *Information and Liaison Bulletin*, No. 34-35-36 (Jan.-Feb.-Mar., 1988), pp. 2-3.

40. The following citations were taken from Adnan Kahveci, "On the Question of Ethnic Problems in Turkey," *Turkish Daily News*, June 2, 1987, p. 6.

41. Kahveci failed to add, of course, that this lack of ethnic discrimination only applied as long as an ethnic Kurd denied his heritage and accepted his role as a political Turk.

42. Cited in Institut Kurde de Paris, *Information and Liaison Bulletin*, No. 43-44-45 (Oct.-Nov.-Dec., 1988), p. 2.

43. Cited in U.S. Helsinki Watch Committee, *Paying the Price*, p. 65.

44. Cited in *Turkey Briefing* (Britain), May 1989.

# 5

# Birth of the PKK
## and Other Kurdish Parties

The *Partia Karkaren Kurdistan* (PKK) or the Kurdish Workers Party is the most violent, radical, and successful Kurdish movement to emerge in Turkey in many years. Its origins can be traced to a meeting of a Dev Genc[1] (Revolutionary Youth) branch of several Kurdish, and a few Turkish, university students at a small house in the Tuzlucayir district of Ankara in 1974. Abdullah (Apo) Ocalan, a dropout from the Political Science Faculty of Ankara University, was their leader from the beginning. Accordingly, although it was first called the "Ankara Democratic Patriotic Association of Higher Education," the group soon came to be known popularly as "Apocus," or followers of Apo, a word which also meant "uncle"[2] or, according to the *Briefing Study*,[3] "*dede*" (holy figure) in Kurdish. These connotations were to be carefully exploited by Ocalan.

According to the *Briefing Study*, there were only eleven persons present at this first meeting: Abdullah Ocalan, Cemil Bayik, Kesire Yildirim, Ali Ozer, Musa Erdogan, Ismet Kilic, Hasan Asgar Gurgoze, Kemal Pir, Kamer Ozkan, Baki Karer, and Ali Haydar (Fuat) Kaytan. Yildirim, apparently the only female member of this association, was at first the fiancee of another leading militant, Ismet Dogru. She left him to marry Ocalan and become for many years one of his closest confidants. She also played an important role in establishing relations with the Soviet Culture Center in Damascus, thus enabling terrorist defectors from Turkey to be indoctrinated by Soviet-trained agents. In 1988, however, she left Ocalan to join a breakaway group in Western Europe.

Baki Karer broke with Ocalan in the fall of 1985, and also travelled to Western Europe to oppose Ocalan. Ali Haydar (Fuat) Kaytan was arrested in West Germany in January 1989, at which time he was identified as a member of the Central Committee of the PKK.[4]

According to a member of the group who later left it, there were only seven members present at this first meeting in Ankara. With the exception of Ocalan, Bayik, and Pir this list is different from the one given above: Abdullah Ocalan, Haki Karaer, Kemal Pir, Mehmet Hayri Durmus, Mazlum Dogan, Cemil Bayik, and Sahin Donmez. Pir and Durmus died in a hunger strike at the Diyarbakir prison in 1982, while Dogan, a former student in the Economics Department of Hacettepe University in Ankara who came from Elazig, supposedly committed suicide at that notorious prison in the same year. Karaer was killed by another Kurdish organization three years later, while Donmez became an informer for the state. (See below.) In possible explanation for these two partially different lists of founding members, one might conjecture that different people might have been present at different meetings, all of which later came to be looked upon as the constitutive meeting of the group.

According to Martin van Bruinessen, one of the most knowledge-able scholars of Kurdish affairs,[5] Ocalan's group, compared to various other Kurdish associations at that time, was "the only organization whose members were drawn almost exclusively from the lowest social classes--the uprooted, half-educated village and small-town youth who knew what it felt like to be oppressed and who wanted action, not ideological sophistication."[6] Bruinessen also noted that Ocalan's group "represents the most marginal sections of Kurdish society, the ones who feel excluded from the country's social and economic develop-ment, [and the] victims of the rural transformation with frustrated expectations."[7] Ocalan offered them "a simple and appropriate theory, and lots of opportunities for action, heroism and martyrdom."[8]

At their first meeting, Ocalan told his followers that the time for a Kurdish independence movement in Turkey had arrived and that their group would be separated from the rest of the Turkish left and other "compromising" Kurdish groups. Further meetings followed in which Ocalan emphasized such ideas as the economic exploitation of the Kurdish areas in Turkey, how the Kurds had different national characteristics such as language, culture, and social structure, and how the Turkish military therefore were invading troops. The Kurds, he continued, had a right to determine their own future. By 1975, the group began political propaganda activities in eastern Anatolia or what it termed "Kurdistan."

Kemal Pir and Cemil Bayik were sent to Gaziantep, Sahin Donmez and Haydar Kaytan went to Tunceli (the site of the major Kurdish revolt in the late 1930s when the province was still known by its Kurdish name "Dersim"), while Ocalan himself returned to his home town, Urfa. Their activities consisted of secret meetings with university students, workers, and local youth.[9] At the same time ideological debates with Turkey's main leftist revolutionary organizations such as Dev Yol[10] (Revolutionary Way) were taking place. Apocus soon earned the reputation of being a violent and narrowly nationalist grouping.

In 1977,[11] Ocalan and his associates met at the Bagcilar district of Diyarbakir, the city in eastern Turkey often considered to be in effect the capital of Turkish Kurdistan. There they produced a program draft which was in time widely distributed throughout Turkey under the title of *Kurdistan Devriminin Yolu* or the Path of the Kurdish Revolution.[12]

The Program declared that Kurdistan had become "a classic colonial country colonized separately by Iran, Iraq, Turkey and Syria." (Interestingly the small Kurdish area in the Soviet Union was not mentioned.) "The development of colonialist capitalism in Kurdistan . . . was built upon the plunder and exploitation of the country's resources," and "in the capitalist stage, the Turks are in the forefront of the forces colonising Kurdistan." To overcome the reaction to this situation, the Turkish government had implemented "a harsh cultural policy and an intense campaign of assimilation."

In the present situation "the feudal landowners . . . are collaborating closely with colonialist capitalism" and are "taking the form of becoming comprador and collaborationist bourgeois, thus involving a profound repudiation of the nation." Moreover "the situation of the peasantry has become even worse" because "the introduction of the tractor and the concentration of land in certain hands has led to great unemployment." In addition "intellectual strata are . . . developing in an atmosphere of Turkish language and culture. Most of these intellectuals are denying their nation and considering themselves Turks rather than Kurds."

The final part of the PKK Program explained that the "Kurdistan revolution . . . has two aspects: national and democratic." The former looked to the establishment of an independent Kurdistan and was a prerequisite to the attainment of further objectives. The second, democratic aspect of the revolution would be "to clear away the contradictions in society left over from the Middle Ages." Specifically mentioned were "feudal and comprador exploitation, tribalism, religious sectarianism and the slave-like dependence of women." Socialism would be "the first stage of this [new] society," while "establishing the classless society" the final goal.

In regards to "the question of leadership" the Program declared "that the fundamental force of the revolution will be the worker-peasant alliance." The proletariat would provide "the ideological, political and organisational leadership," while the peasantry would constitute the "main force" of the "popular army." Victory would be achieved "through the mobilisation of the broad forces of the people and a long-term struggle." Given "the colonialists' extremely harsh repression . . . the methods of struggle are of necessity based to a large extent on violence." "Defeatist approaches which do not aim to smash the colonial yoke of the Republic of Turkey and propose things like 'regional autonomy,'" would be exposed. The Program added, however, that "this does not mean that other methods of struggle will not be used given suitable concrete conditions."

The revolution would ensure that a number of specific "tasks" would be accomplished. (1) "All land belonging to landowners, except for patriotic elements, will be confiscated, nationalised and distributed free to peasants having little land." (2) "All the debts of poor peasants to usurers and banks will be canceled." (3) "The economy will be directed through central planning [and] priority will be given to the development of nationalised heavy industry." (4) "One of the Kurdish dialects will be encouraged to develop into the national language." (5) "The workers'-peasants' government . . . will . . . provide no military bases or privileges to any other country. (6) "To support the unity of Kurdistan . . . efforts will be made to ensure the closest possible support and solidarity among the revolutionary forces fighting in every section," i. e. Iraq, Iran, and Syria. (7) "Friendship with the socialist countries, alliance with the National Liberation Movements and solidarity with the working class movement and democratic trends in every part of the world will be established."

Sahin Donmez, who later became a "repentant" or informer for the government, explained that "the best method to spread Marxist-Leninist ideology was "armed propaganda."[13] This concept, which was popular among several radical, leftist groups in the 1970s, meant to carry out attacks that would attract public attention to the group and its cause. Violence was necessary to break the chain of treachery against the Kurdish cause.

Illustrating its belief and emphasis on violence, Ocalan's group has written that "violence . . . will in Kurdistan not only be the midwife assisting in the delivery [of a new society] but will create everything anew. Revolutionary violence has to play this role in Kurdistan, and it will, we say, assume the form of revolutionary revenge."[14] Only contempt was offered for those who did not agree: "Pseudo-socialist sermons will not save us any better than the religious sermons that they have come to replace."[15]

On May 18, 1977, Haki Karaer, one of the founding members of Apocus, was killed in Gaziantep by a Kurdish organization called the "*Isterkasor*" or the Red Star. Believing Karaer's death to be either some kind of a plot or at least the result of poor security measures, the Gaziantep branch of Apocus decided to break off from the organization. Thus a new splinter group known as "*Tekosin*" was established. Its first two leaders--Ali Yaylacik and Mehmet Uzun--however, were executed by Ocalan's group. Many remember this early incident as proof of Ocalan's willingness to use violence and terrorism.

In the 1970s, however, security forces of the state were not seen as a target since to do so would endanger the preparations or organizational structure of Apocus. As a result, most of the violence was directed against state collaborators, militants of the rightist Idealist Youths, members of tribes known to be on friendly terms with the Turkish government, and even leftist groups which opposed Apo's policies. Mounting tensions, for example, occurred between Apocus and the radical, leftist Dev Yol in the Diyarbakir Ofis district where an ideological debate between leaders of the two groups almost led to bloodshed in the streets. By this time then, Ocalan decided it was appropriate to establish a formal party.

*PKK Established.*--On November 27, 1978, Ocalan and his supporters met at the house of "Seyfettin" (supposedly one of the few "patriotic" landlords who supported them) in the village of Fis in the Lice township of Diyarbakir to establish the PKK. The decision was taken to sign all communiques with this new name, instead of the earlier terms that had been used, "National Liberation Army" or "Kurdistan Revolutionaries." Seven persons were named to the party's first Central Committee: Abdullah Ocalan (General Secretary), Kesire

Yildirim, Sahin Donmez, Cemil Bayik, Mehmet Karasungur, Mazlum Dogan, and Mehmet Hayi Durmus. Karasungur was the only one who had not been listed as present at the initial meeting of Apocus in 1974. Dogan was put in charge of printing *Serxwebun* (Independence), the party's official journal.

To announce the establishment of the PKK, an armed propaganda action in the form of an assassination was decided upon. Mehmet Celal Bucak, a Justice Party chieftain and landlord in the Siverek district, was the intended victim. He was accused of terrorizing the countryside with bandits under his employment and of extorting cash and property from the local peasants. To the PKK, therefore, Bucak epitomized the ideal of a government "collaborator."

When the attempt failed, a bloody feud started between Bucak's supporters (including some elements of the state's authority) and the PKK. Conflicts broke out elsewhere too against "fascist circles" and armed militias of feudal landlords in Hilvan and Siverek, as well as the *Devrimci Halkin Birligi* (Revolutionary Unity of the People), the *Halkin Kurtulusu* (Liberation of the People), and the DDKD (Revolutionary Democratic Cultural Associations). The PKK branded its latter three opponents as "social chauvinists" and "nationalist reformists." In the province of Mardin the PKK attacked the KUK (National Liberation of Kurdistan), a group that had established deep roots there among most of the different social elements.

According to Baki Karer, one of the original members of Apocus who later broke from the group in 1985, the PKK would kill one member of a particular tribe and make it seem as if it had been done by Bucak's men to win the support of that tribe. Karer also accused Ocalan of systematically carrying out similar other such bloody acts, claiming that more than twenty persons from the PKK's own membership were murdered for various reasons.[16] Bruinessen concluded, however, that: "There was also a definite aspect of class struggle to these conflicts. . . . Much of the PKK's violence was directed against the haves in the name of the have-nots."[17]

During the 1978-1980 period, PKK party work mainly focused on three regions: (1) Gaziantep, Kahramanmaras, and Malatya, (2) Urfa, Diyarbakir and Mardin, and (3) Elazig, Tunceli, and Bingol. The secretary of each one of these three regions was also a member of the PKK's Central Committee. There were also subcommittees corresponding to the provincial level and local committees operating under them. Although the party's Central Committee supposedly controlled armed actions, the regional committees and their provincial subcommittees apparently possessed a sizable amount of lecway.

In some of the districts the PKK claimed as "liberated areas," a few of the Kurdish villagers probably looked upon it as their liberators. As "peoples' courts" dealt out "revolutionary justice," efforts also were made to break out of what had previously always been a purely illegal level of operation. Semi-legal students and workers organizations were now created to provide some grassroots support for the party. Most Turkish Kurds, however, seemed to resent the PKK's violent tactics and began to view it as brutal, reckless, and irresponsible.

For finances the PKK turned increasingly to bank robberies and stealing from jewelers or others. Given its location on Turkey's southeastern border with Iran, Iraq, and Syria, the PKK was also able to turn to arms and narcotics smuggling.[18] With the escalating anarchy in Turkey at this time, the party was able to operate with increasing impunity.

## Other Kurdish Groups

A number of other Kurdish political organizations--sometimes ephemeral, always subject to splintering, and thus often confusing to analyze--emerged in the ferment of the mid-1970s.[19] This was a time of great social, as well as political, tensions. Kurdish migrations to the cities of western Turkey had attained prodigious levels during the 1960s and continued without abatement into the 1970s. Politicized in their closed *gecekondus* (shanty towns), this new generation, when parts of it returned to the Kurdish areas in the East, became the primary catalyst for the Kurdish movements that were developing. Ocalan's PKK, for example, in part owed its creation to this situation.

Politically, the relatively liberal atmosphere of the times, coupled with the increasing political paralysis analyzed above in Chapter 3, allowed this renewed Kurdish consciousness to express itself. When the traditional Turkish political parties, as well as the new Turkish left, largely proved unsympathetic,a number of explicitly Kurdish organizations began to appear. An attempt to revive the old Revolutionary Cultural Society of the East (DDKO), a Kurdish organization described above in Chapter 2, under the title Revolutionary Democratic Cultural Associations (DDKD), however, failed. Other movements soon followed.

*SPTK.*--The Socialist Party of Turkish Kurdistan (SPTK) was, in effect, established in 1974 by some members of the discontinued Turkish Workers Party. Until its formal creation in 1979, the SPTK was known as *Riya Azadi* (The Road to Freedom) in Kurdish or *Ozgurluk Yolu* in Turkish after its monthly journal which lasted from 1975 until its suppression early in 1979. Led by its General Secretary, Kemal Burkay, the party had a small urban following of workers and intellectuals who advocated moderate socialist and nationalist goals, and possessed some influence in such trade and teachers unions as TOB DER and TUM DER. Before the 1980 military intervention, its militants were involved in armed actions in and around Van. Indeed, as mentioned above in Chapter 4, Mehdi Zana, the former mayor of the southeastern Anatolian city of Diyarbakir, was sentenced to a thirty-two year prison term in 1982, for supposedly carrying out activities under the purview of the SPTK.

"Our Party is the politic organization of the working class and poor farmers of Kurdistan," stated the program of the SPTK.[20] The revolution it foresaw would come in two stages: Because "Kurdistan has not got its national independence yet and done away with feudalism, the character of the revolutionary stage facing the Kurdish people is the national democratic revolution. This revolution is going to take the colonial fetters off the people, wipe out the foreign domination, and liberate the Kurds." Continuing, the program declared: "Our Party knows very well that only socialism can put an end to exploitation and backwardness." Thus, "the national democratic revolution should be brought to perfection by the socialist revolution."

To help achieve these revolutions, the "SPTK finds it necessary to establish a United National Democratic Front." This Front "admits all progressive and democratic people, irrespective of their class background, as long as they should be anti-imperialist, anti-colonial and anti-feudal." Accordingly, the SPTK cooperated with several other Kurdish groups, but remained implacably opposed to the PKK. There even were armed clashes between the two before 1980.

Interestingly enough the SPTK believed that the Kurds "can live together with the Turkish people, under a democratic system, if the principles of equality are observed." Thus "there will be set up either a federation in Turkey or the Kurdish people will establish their own independent state. . . . Time and the historical development will tell."

The needs of non-Turkish Kurds were also seen as important. "Our Party should help the struggle of the Kurdish people in the other parts of Kurdistan as well." The program of the party declared that "if Turkish Kurdistan is liberated earlier, we shall do our best to help the liberation of the other parts; and when two or three parts are liberated, we shall do our best to unite them."

On the international front, the SPTK took a moderately pro-Soviet and anti-American position, probably largely because the Turkish government was a NATO ally of the United States and the Soviet Union was their perceived opponent. "Our Party . . . supports the serious efforts of the Soviet Union and the other socialist countries toward the general disarmament . . . [and] the peace-movements against the attempts of the USA and the other imperialistic powers to locate new middle-range missiles." In addition, the SPTK felt "the USSR helps the liberation struggle of the Afghan people" and was in favor of Turkey "leaving NATO."

Since the 1980 military coup, a number of the members of the SPTK have been imprisoned. Others have gone into exile abroad. Kemal Burkay, for example, has lived in Sweden for a number of years.

*Revolutionary Democrats.*--The checkered fortunes of the originally conservative, nationalistic, and pro-Barzani Kurdish Democratic Party of Turkey (KDPT) that was created by Faik Bucak in 1965 were traced above in Chapter 2. After the Party underwent a number of divisions in the late 1960s and early 1970s, a group of the more leftist sympathizers of the slain Shivan won control of some of the largest branches of the DDKD and began to use that organization's name, "Revolutionary Democrats." It claimed to be Marxist and attempted to gain the support of the pro-Soviet Turkish Communist Party. Its publications appealed mostly to intellectuals and the youth, but its membership included even "feudal" elements. According to Bruinessen, the Revolutionary Democrats became the largest Kurdish organization by the late 1970s and claimed to have some forty branches with about 50,000 members.[21]

*PPKK.*--Closely associated with the Revolutionary Democrats was the Kurdish Vanguard Workers Party (PPKK), generally known as *Pesheng* (Vanguard). The PPKK called for an independent republic of Kurdistan, saw itself as struggling for the social and economic rights of the workers and peasants, and tended to be pro-Soviet. Reduced by the arrests which followed the military coup of September 1980, as well as a split over party organization between its European and Kurdistan parts in 1982, the PPKK supposedly now enjoys close relations with the SPTK and the KUK (see below). Its current Secretary-General, Serhad Dicle, spoke in the name of Tevger, a broad alliance of some eight Kurdish groups, at a meeting in Stockholm, Sweden in January, 1989.

*KUK*.--The fortunes of the slain Sait Elchi and his KDPT faction were discussed above in Chapter 2. Their remnants continued for a period as little more than an appendage of Mullah Mustafa Barzani's Iraqi KDP. After the collapse of Barzani's rebellion in 1975, however, some of its younger and more militant members eventually organized themselves as the National Liberation of Kurdistan (KUK) in 1977. By the late 1970s, this group had put down strong roots in the southeastern Turkish province of Mardin which lies near both the Syrian and Iraqi borders. There it had violent confrontations with the PKK.

The KUK supported the "Provisional Leadership" of the Iraqi KDP, led in the 1980s by Barzani's son, Massoud, and also associated itself with the SPTK in a theoretical United Democratic Front in the early 1980s. Interestingly enough, the "CIA Report" on the Kurds written in 1979, termed the KUK one of the "two . . . more important [Kurdish] covert groups" in Turkey.[22]

*Rizgari*.--Another Marxist group grew up in 1976 around the publishing house Komal and became known by the name of its journal, *Rizgari* (Liberation), which was banned after its second issue. Contrary to the position of the *Ozgurluk Yolu* group (SPTK), *Rizgari* did not support Bulent Ecevit's RPP in the 1977 national elections, arguing that as a colonized people, the Kurds could expect little from the Turks. Kurdish liberation would be won by a socialist revolution led by the Kurdish proletariat. In the late 1970s, *Rizgari* was "credited with organising street riots in Diyarbekir."[23]

*Ala Rizgari*.--Ideological and personal conflicts led to a split in *Rizgari* in 1979, and still another splinter group, *Ala Rizgari* (Flag of Liberation) was formed. Sometimes described as "Trotskyist," this new organization was mostly non-violent, and more flexible in its political position and censorious of the Soviet Union than was *Rizgari*.

*Kawa.*--This violent, anti-Soviet, Maoist group was named for a legendary Iranian blacksmith who supposedly rebelled against the tyrant, Dehak, during the time of the ancient Persian Empire. The Kurdish and Iranian new-year celebration of this event at the beginning of spring is called *Newroz*, and, since 1984, has annually become the signal for a new PKK offensive in southeastern Turkey. (See Chapter 6 below.) Kawa itself was established in 1976, but split over arguments concerning China's "Three World" theory two years later.

Shortly after the military came to power in 1980, Kawa made national headlines when more than one hundred rocket launchers were unearthed in Nusaybin near the Syrian border. Suat Oraz, a member of Kawa, confessed that they had been smuggled into Turkey from Syria as a gift from the Iraqi Kurdish leader, Celal Talabani.[24]

Although Bruinessen wrote that Kawa "never gained much following outside some student circles,"[25] an independent Turkish source has claimed that it "was engaged in more violent acts than others, with the exception of [the] PKK."[26] The CIA concurred with this assessment by asserting Kawa was one of the "two . . . more important [Kurdish] covert groups."[27] Based on events subsequent to the writing of the "CIA Report" and since the seemingly minor KUK was the other Kurdish "covert group" termed "important" by the CIA, it seems clear that Bruinessen's assessment of Kawa is more accurate.

## The 1980 Coup

All of this Kurdish activity in Turkey, of course, was simply a small part of the much larger terrorism and anarchy, described above in Chapter 3, that was going on throughout the country in the late 1970s. Finally on September 12, 1980, the Turkish military stepped in and called a halt to the headlong rush to destruction. Apparently anticipating the coup, Abdullah (Apo) Ocalan himself withdrew to Syria in time to escape capture. He has remained there ever since.

According to its own figures, General Evren's new military government apprehended and placed on trial almost 20,000 suspects as of March 31, 1983.[28] More than 15,000 of them were charged with membership in left-wing terrorist organizations, while similar right-wing groups accounted for less than 1,000. Only 3,177 were accused of "separatist activities," illustrating how Kurdish separatism at that time did not seem to be such a major threat. (Given the PKK's resurgence after 1984, some wonder if the government did not err.)

PKK suspects numbered 1,790, by far the largest of the "separatist" groups. Members of the SPTK and *Tekosin* (a breakaway PKK group mentioned above) accounted for 637 of the accused, 459 came from Kawa, and the rest from various other groups including *Rizgari*, *Ala Rizgari*, and KUK. According to other reports, by 1981, more than 2,000 alleged PKK members were in prison, while 447 were put on mass trial and accused of forming "armed gangs" to "annex" southeastern Turkey.[29]

The formal indictment claimed that the PKK was a "clandestine separatist organisation . . . aspiring to establish a Marxist-Leninist state in Eastern and Southeastern Anatolia after an armed struggle."[30] Since beginning its violent campaign, the Party had murdered 243 people. Most of the defendants were young (between 18-25), poorly educated workers, farmers, or shepherds, and unemployed.

Many of the accused were given lengthy prison terms, while a few were sentenced to death. Although some--such as Mehmet Hayri Durmus, Kemal Pir, and Mazlum Dogan--were members of the PKK's top echelon, most of the Party's leaders managed to get out of the country. At the time, however, it appeared that the state had broken the backbone of Kurdish separatism.

### Notes

1.   Dev Genc was a radical, leftist student organization in the 1970s which helped set the background for much of the leftist violence of that time. See Chapter 3 above.

2.   Martin van Bruinessen, "Between Guerrilla War and Political Murder: The Workers' Party of Kurdistan," *Middle East Report*, No. 153 (July-Aug. 1988), p. 42.

3.   The independent Turkish weekly, *Briefing*, published a detailed analysis of the PKK over a period of several weeks during the summer of 1988. The series was written by Ismet G. Imset, the Diplomatic News Editor of *Briefing*, and entitled: "PKK: The Deception of Terror," hereafter referred to as the *Briefing Study*. Although Imset himself warned that one had to be careful in analyzing the information "considering the amount of misinformation passed on," his analysis is an invaluable source of information on the PKK, especially when it is correlated with other available data. Much of my following analysis about earlier events in the PKK's history is

taken from this source. I have so indicated in the text and a number of my notes, but to do so on every occasion seemed unnecessarily pedantic and repetitious.

4. "F. Almanya'da PKK'ya Darbe," *Milliyet*, Jan. 2, 1989.

5. M.M. van Bruinessen, *Agha, Shaikh and State: On the Social and Political Organization of Kurdistan* (Utrecht, The Netherlands: University of Utrecht, 1978) is possibly the best study available on the Kurds. Also see Thomas Bois and Vladimir Minorsky, "Kurds, Kurdistan," *The Encyclopedia of Islam* (new edition), V, 1981, 438-86.

6. Bruinessen, "Workers' Party of Kurdistan," p. 41.

7. *Ibid.*, p. 42.

8. *Ibid.*

9. *Briefing Study.*

10. Dev Yol was a radical, leftist group formed from the previously mentioned Dev Genc. See Chapter 3 above.

11. Bruinessen says "1978." "Workers' Party of Kurdistan," p. 42.

12. The following citations are taken from Serxwebun [PKK], "Programme," Feb. 1983, an English-language translation published in Cologne, West Germany.

13. *Briefing Study.*

14. Cited in Bruinessen, "Workers' Party of Kurdistan," p. 50n14.

15. Cited in *ibid.*

16. *Ibid.*, pp. 42, 46n6.

17. Cited in *ibid.*, p. 42.

18. See Mark S. Steinitz, "Insurgents, Terrorists and the Drug Trade," *The Washington Quarterly*, (Fall 1985), p. 145.

19. One *New York Times* report declared that there were "a dozen Kurdish underground groups in Turkey" (Sept. 9, 1979, p. 3), while another said there were "about 10" (June 11, 1980, p. A3). A *Christian Science Monitor* article stated that there were "16 different Kurdish underground organizations" (Aug. 28, 1979, p. 4), while an analysis for the Institute for the Study of Conflict in London asserted: "Turkish Kurdistan . . . has about 15 small violently active clandestine groups." Richard Sims, *Kurdistan: The Search for Recognition*, No. 124 (London: The Institute for the Study of Conflict, 1980), p. 17.

20. The following analysis and citations are based on three SPTK documents: "The Socialist Party of Turkish Kurdistan," May 1982; "A Report of the Address by Kemal Burkay, General Secretary of the Socialist Party of Turkey Kurdistan, to the Labour Movement Conference on Turkey Held 22nd September, 1984, at the Headquarters of the NUR," n. d.; and "Socialist Party of Turkish Kurdistan (SPTK), Appeal to the Delegates of the 23rd General Conference of the UNESCO, Sofia/Bulgaria," Oct. 8, 1985.

21. See Martin van Bruinessen, "The Kurds in Turkey," *MERIP Reports*, No. 121 (Feb. 1984), pp. 10-11.

22. National Foreign Assessment Center (U.S. Central Intelligence Agency), *The Kurdish Problem in Perspective* (Aug. 1979), p. 28.

23. Sims, *Kurdistan: Search for Recognition*, p. 17.

24. "The Internal Threat, 1920-1984," *Briefing* (Ankara), Oct. 8, 1984, p. 14.

25. Bruinessen, "Kurds in Turkey," p. 10.

26. *Briefing* (Ankara), Oct. 8, 1984, p. 14.

27. *Kurdish Problem in Perspective*, p. 28.

28. *Briefing Study*. Also see the text and figures respectively in the book and report published by Evren's new government: *12 September in Turkey: Before and After* (Ankara: Ongun Kardesler Printing House, 1982), pp. 245-50; and *Anarchy and Terrorism in Turkey* [1982], pp. 40, 58, 60, and 74.

29. This and the following analysis is largely based on Marvine Howe, "Turkey Opens Campaign Against Kurdish Rebels," *New York Times*, Apr. 1, 1981, p. A9; Metin Munir, "447 Turkish Kurds Are Put on Trial for Separatist Violence," *Washington Post*, Apr. 14, 1981; and Kenneth Mackenzie, "Turkish Extremists Face Mass Trials," *Jerusalem Post*, Apr. 24, 1981, p. 13.

30. Cited in *12 September*, p. 249.

# 6

## Revival of the PKK

Most members of the PKK who managed to escape after the military coup in Turkey gathered in Syria,[1] although other sources indicate that important elements also found refuge in Iraq and Iran.[2] Abdullah (Apo) Ocalan, the leader of the PKK, lived in a district of Damascus normally off limits to foreigners. He acquired a villa in that city, travelled about in a red Mercedes provided by the Syrians, and enjoyed the protection of bodyguards from that state.

In July 1981, the PKK held its first congress at the Lebanese-Syrian border. The political report issued by the congress criticized the party for its tactics and organizational activities before the Turkish coup and admitted that armed clashes that had taken place then with certain other Kurdish groups, such as the KUK, were a mistake. A period of reorganization and broad political and military training were called for. At the same time the PKK expanded its contacts in western Europe with various Kurdish groups in exile. This was done particularly in Sweden and West Germany. (See Chapter 7 below.)

By 1982 preparations were deemed adequate to hold the party's second congress, again in Syrian territory. Although Ocalan had apparently managed to alienate several members of the original Central Committee, he emerged in full control. Indeed one of his main opponents was supposedly imprisoned, tortured into signing a confession of immoral conduct, and finally executed.[3]

The political program of the second congress declared that the Kurdish revolution would begin with weak forces against a strong enemy in a semi-feudal colony as a national war of liberation or long-term popular war. The armed struggle in Kurdistan would depend on targets of political struggle. Three stages of this struggle were identified:    (1) strategic defense, (2) balance of forces, and (3) strategic attack period.

The first phase of strategic defense was expected to last until 1995.[4] It would involve armed propaganda activities, attacks against state collaborators, and the preparation of an armed movement. The second phase of a balance of forces was projected for the period 1995-2000. This stage consisted of the creation of liberated zones in which the PKK could hide and prepare for action, an alliance with the Turkish armed, radical left, the ability to prevent the state from launching serious blows to the party, and the establishment of armed forces adequate for carrying out a large-scale guerrilla war. Finally the third stage of strategic attack would see the abandonment of "active defense" in favor of a full scale offensive that would in effect amount to a popular uprising in the southeast after 2000. As of this writing (early 1990), the PKK, despite many setbacks, had clearly achieved the goals of the first stage and was already pursuing those of the second.

After its second congress in 1982, the PKK sent its first reconnaissance groups back into Turkish territory. This proved simple enough to accomplish since border security measures were quite lax then, and the difficult terrain provided added security. Those agents entering Turkey were ordered to find hide-outs in the mountains, locate places where supplies could be hidden, and establish contact with potential supporters in the villages. They also were to gather data on the Turkish forces and their local collaborators. The groundwork for future guerrilla warfare was being established.

Early in 1983, Turkish intelligence sources identified a force of some 12,000 Kurdish guerrillas in an area stretching approximately seventy kilometers along the Turkish-Iraqi frontier.[5] Although most of the Kurds belonged to the Iraqi Kurdish Democratic Party (KDP), now led by Massoud Barzani since the death of his famous father Mulla Mustafa Barzani in 1979, some of them were PKK fighters. Because the Iraqi troops were tied down by their war with Iran, the Kurds were free to do what they pleased in the rugged border area.

In May 1983, these PKK militants ambushed a Turkish army unit, killing three soldiers and wounding an officer. The Turkish authorities took the matter very seriously, and, with the permission of Iraq, launched the first of many subsequent strikes over the border. According to the Iraqi Ambassador in Ankara, the Turks captured some 2000 "separatists,"[6] while other sources claim that several hundred Kurds were killed.[7] Martin van Bruinessen, however, a well-connected observer of Kurdish affairs, declared that since the Kurds immediately fled from their camps, the Turks finally had to withdraw without capturing or killing anyone.[8]

Be that as it may it is clear that the Turkish strike of May 1983 failed to end PKK activity. In January 1984, for example, both Radio Ankara and the British Broadcasting Company reported that twenty PKK guerrillas, who had been involved in armed robberies, had been captured in the southeastern region of Turkey centering around Adana, Icel, Kahramanmaras, Gaziantep, Adiyaman, and Hatay.

Important, even indispensable, for these activities, were contacts made with other organizations. Under interrogation PKK members have related how Palestinians with Soviet training instructed them in camps under Syrian control. (See below in Chapter 7.) In July 1983, the PKK secured a valuable alliance when it signed a protocol with Massoud Barzani's KDP operating in northern Iraq. Founded in 1946 by Massoud's legendary father, Mulla Mustafa Barzani, the Iraqi KDP could put maybe 10,000 or more *peshmergas* (those who court death) or fighters into the field. Barzani sought the alliance because his earlier one with the KUK was no longer operative given that group's decline after the Turkish military crackdown in 1980. A relationship with another viable Kurdish organization from Turkey was deemed valuable for the furtherance of the KDP's ambitions in Iraq.

Under their accord the KDP and the PKK agreed upon a unified commitment against "every kind of imperialism, with American imperialism at the top of the list, and the struggle against the plans and plots of imperialism in the region."[9] The two parties also committed themselves to "cooperation with other revolutionary forces in the region and the creation of new alliances." Another provision of their protocol emphasized that the struggle "should depend on the force of the Kurdish people." Article 10 of the agreement stated that neither party should interfere in the internal affairs of the other or commit actions that could damage the other. The eleventh and final article of their "Principles of Solidarity" declared that if one of them made a mistake in implementing their alliance and a warning from the other was ignored, then their alliance could be terminated.

At first the accord worked well for both parties. PKK militants being trained in Syrian and Lebanese camps were slowly moved to northern Iraq where new camps were now established at such places as Haftanin and Lejno Zaho. PKK leaders apparently travelled mostly through Tehran and then to northern Iraq, while the "foot soldiers" moved from Syria as armed groups over the Turkish border near Silopi and Cizre. From there they travelled on foot over the Silopi-Sarnak-Uludere path into northern Iraq.

Soon the Lolan camp, located in the triangle of land where Turkey, Iran, and Iraq meet, became the PKK's largest base in its newly found sanctuary. This camp also contained the PKK press and publications center, as well as the KDP's headquarters and clandestine radio stations. In addition the PKK used camps at Lak-1, Kuvvet Barzan, and Miroz which were also scattered around the border with Turkey.

At this time Ocalan apparently carried out a purge against such PKK members as M. Resul Altinok (said to have been a member of the party's central committee), Saime Askin, Cemil Efeturk, Ibrahim Halik, Ayten Yildirim, Besil Yildiz, Sabahattin Ali, Inanc Haymanali, M. Ali Cetiner, and Yasar Organ. Most of these individuals were reportedly tortured and forced to confess that they were traitors. Eventually they were executed. The time had now arrived for the PKK to launch an attack within Turkey that would attract international attention.

### Renewed Struggle

On August 15, 1984, the PKK announced the establishment of the *Hazen Rizgariya Kurdistan* (HRK) or Kurdistan Freedom Brigades by making two, well-coordinated attacks on Eruh and Semdinli, villages in southeastern Turkey separated by rugged, mountainous terrain and more than 200 miles apart. In each of these two attacks about forty guerrillas entered the village and held it for one hour. Eyewitnesses stated that the insurgents were well organized and even brought medical teams with them. Although the Turkish army attempted to react, the partisans were able to escape.

Turkish authorities have described the HRK as "a duplicate of the Vietcong."[10] Its structure was based on a 3-3 military system: three squads constituted a team; three teams formed a company, etc. Three units of the HRK were established and named: (1) March 21 Armed Propaganda Unit, (2) July 14 Armed Propaganda Unit, and (3) May 18 Armed Propaganda Unit. The first-named unit was active in Hakkari during 1984, but no further data were listed for the other two.

Duran (Abbas) Kalkan was named the Secretary-General of the Council of the HRK. Although he was identified as the "number two" person in the PKK in 1988, he reportedly broke with Ocalan in that year over violence against Kurdish villages which he believed hurt the party's recruitment efforts.[11] He was arrested in West Germany at the beginning of 1989.[12]

The other members of the Council of the HRK were: Ali (Cemal) Omurcan, Halil (Abu-Bakr) Atac, Mahsun or Mazlum (Agit) Korkmaz, Halil Kaya (Kor Cemal), Sabri (Hassan) Ok, Sah (Shehmuz) Ismail, and Abdullah Ekinci (Esref or Bingollu Ali). Of these persons, Korkmaz posthumously gained the most fame. (See below.)

Despite its apparent success, the PKK was able to launch nothing more than hit-and-run attacks for the rest of 1984. Indeed the Turks were able to counter by striking against PKK bases in northern Iraq in an action referred to as "Operation Sun" during the last week in October. Reports at that time stated that there were about 400 PKK guerrillas along with some 17,000 KDP *peshmergas* in the area.[13] Although the Minister of the Interior, Yildirim Akbulut, reported to the Turkish Parliament in November 1984 that Turkish security forces had "killed 14 terrorists and captured 3 others during operations in southeastern Turkey,"[14] nothing conclusive was accomplished. By December 1984, the prominent members of the HRK had been withdrawn from Turkey to their camps in northern Iraq. A period of evaluation began.

According to the PKK publication *Serxwebun*, "a warfare which would rapidly become a guerrilla war in Central Kurdistan will begin, and, in the possible areas where developments are achieved, local rebellions will be started."[15] Central Kurdistan (Hakkari, Van, and Siirt) was chosen because "in this area, the control by the enemy is weak compared to that in north-west Kurdistan, and its geography consists of mountains and rugged terrain." Therefore, concluded the PKK, "among the people, natural patriotism [for the Kurds] is wide-spread and the masses are sympathetic to the struggle for their national liberation, and willing to participate in the resistance and support it."

The PKK also decided that in the following May (1985) an operation would be launched to commemorate the "revolutionary martyrs." This would be followed in the July-September period with a "Red Resistance Operation" that would become an "Operation to Strengthen the Party" in November. These decisions heralded the inception of a new popular front or military flank within the PKK, and on May 21, 1985, the creation of the Kurdistan National Liberation Front or ERNK (Cephe) was announced. Mazlum Korkmaz, described as "Ocalan's right-hand man," was named as its first commander. The exact relationship between the previously created HRK and the new ERNK, however, was not clear.

Be that as it may determined infiltrations across the Iraqi border began again in the spring of 1985. Similar spring offensives, timed to coincide with the Kurdish new year or *Newroz*, which takes place in the spring, were to become an annual affair. (Spring also, of course, is when it becomes possible to launch military campaigns again after the long, forced hiatus of winter.) The offensive in 1985, however, did not prove very successful. By the later part of the year *Serxwebun* admitted that "everything had to start all over again."[16]

A new offensive during the following year apparently brought some of the success the PKK was seeking. Indeed the PKK was to mark 1986 as the "year of great advances."[17] Mahsun (Mazlum) Korkmaz, the commander of the ERNK, however, was killed by Turkish troops at the beginning of that year's offensive in March 1986. The PKK's Mahsun Korkmaz Military Academy in the Syrian-controlled Bekaa Valley of Lebanon was named after him. According to Kemal Emluk, a seventeen-year-old PKK militant who had been active in the Eruh region before he surrendered to the police in Denizli, this Academy "occupies a space of about 10 thousand square meters and consists of four buildings, one of which is a PKK prison."[18]

The PKK struck its most significant blow to that time in a particularly bold attack that killed twelve members of the Ortabag Border Gendarme Battalion near Uludere, a district of Hakkari province, on August 13, 1986. The party billed this as a major victory of armed propaganda in that it called the attention of the world to the fact that the PKK was actively expanding its campaign.

In retaliation Turkish air force jets bombed KDP and PKK camps in northern Iraq two days later. At least 150 Kurds (including probably women and children) were killed in the raid.[19] Turkish Prime Minister Turgut Ozal announced that three camps housing 100 guerrillas had been destroyed and declared: "We are determined to follow these rebels to their lairs and smash them." Implicitly affirming charges that fighters from Barzani's KDP were also among the casualties, Ozal added: "Let this [be] a warning to those who shelter the rebels."[20]

Although Barzani threatened to respond, Ankara's firmness was apparently an important factor influencing him to reassess his alliance with the PKK. (See below.) In Europe PKK supporters almost assassinated a Turkish diplomat in Hamburg, and in southeastern Anatolia itself the PKK continued to attack soldiers and civilians, as well as kidnap new recruits. Instability and terror had become a daily condition in the area.

It was under these conditions that the PKK held its third congress in Latakia, Syria from October 25-30, 1986. A number of decisions were taken. "Public relations" were identified as the party's most important problem. Despite the perceived successes, public support was still weak. Neither the HRK nor the ERNK had helped to solve this difficulty. Therefore it was decided to create still another formation which would hopefully be a more powerful organization, the People's Liberation Army of Kurdistan or ARGK.

Such a formation was to be the first step toward establishing a 'people's army' like the Mojahideen Halq militia in Iran. It also implied that the PKK fighters had increased in numbers. A communique prepared on October 30, 1986, announced the establishment of the ARGK in the following words: "In the period ahead for the tactical development to create a guerrilla army from armed propaganda and at the same time setting up the people's army and formally beginning constructive work [sic]."[21] Ocalan declared that the new organization meant that "we have realized our final return to our country. From now on there will be no return abroad. Our mountains and our people are apt for us to settle down there, never to be pulled out again and to expand our roots."[22] In effect, the ARGK was supposed to become the military arm of the PKK. Despite this rhetoric, however, by 1988 not much more was to be heard about the ARGK or for that matter the HRK. On the other hand, numerous military and political actions were to be taken in the name of the ERNK. (See below.)

Another decision taken by the PKK's third congress was to step up its attacks against the village guard system of Kurdish villagers loyal to the regime who had been created in the summer of 1985 and armed to ward off PKK attacks. It was also decided to purchase SAM-type missiles from Syria. The congress looked forward to the "elimination of all enemies" and boldly declared that its campaign would soon enter the next stage by establishing "liberated areas" in Turkish Kurdistan.[23]

In the early months of 1987, the ARGK struck a number of targets within southeastern Anatolia. Many of the victims were women and children who were seen as "collaborators." Others included the village guards who were hit so strongly that the system was brought near to collapse. After PKK raids had killed some thirty-four civilians in the previous month alone, therefore, yet another Turkish strike into northern Iraq occurred on March 4, 1987.[24] According to a former PKK member, Ocalan visited the Mahsun Korkmaz Military Academy on March 8, 1987, to celebrate "World's Women's Day." At that time he inspected his fighters and "was greeted like the commander of an army."[25]

The summer of 1987 witnessed an escalation in PKK attacks and the overall seriousness of the situation. On the night of June 20, the village of Pinarcik in the province of Mardin, some sixteen miles from the Syrian border, was struck. Thirty people were killed including 16 children and 8 women. According to Turkish sources: "It was the worst massacre ever committed by the Kurdish insurgents fighting an undeclared war against the Turkish Republic."[26]

Some 30 more civilians died on July 11, 1987, when the villages of Yuvali and Pecenek, also in Mardin province, were attacked. Summing up the situation, the cover story in one Turkish journal declared:

> For a moment last Thursday, the Turkish state looked helpless and unable to root out the terrorists. . . . The claims of successive Turkish governments over many years that the 'Kurdish question' does not exist has been discredited by events. What looked like a local insurgency, has, since the start of this year escalated into something like a full scale guerrilla war.[27]

Three more raids on the night of August 18-19, 1987, led to 27 further deaths, 25 of them civilian, when the villages of Milan in the Eruh district of Siirt and Isikveren in Uludere, Hakkari (near the Iraqi border) were hit. A military vehicle summoned to this latter scene struck a land mine resulting in the death of two soldiers. Turkish sources were forced to conclude: "Against Turkey's increasing military presence in the troubled region, not much seems to have been done to prevent attacks from taking place."[28] In a striking admission for a state which hitherto officially had denied the very existence of the Kurds, the same report declared "that the PKK has achieved one goal

... bring[ing] the 'Kurdish question' finally to the international platform."[29]

During the summer of 1987, lesser attacks also occurred in Diyarbakir, Yuvali, Tunceli, Bingol, Kars, Hozat, Tunceri, Nusaybin, Gercus, and Caylidere, among others.[30] Turkish sources even began to speculate that "the Kurdish Workers Party is planning to carry out large attacks in major cities,"[31] a threat that, as of the beginning of 1990 at least, has not materialized, probably because of timely arrests of PKK agents in the major cities of western Turkey.

The southeastern Turkish provinces of Mardin, Siirt, and Hakkari were the main targets of the PKK. One government source even referred to them as the "Devil's Triangle" and stated that the PKK seemed to be trying to establish them as a "liberated zone" or "central base."[32] All three provinces bordered either on or near the frontier with Syria, Iraq, and Iran. Indeed the Turkish intelligence claimed that "PKK guerrillas have bases in all three of Turkey's three southern neighbours."[33]

Until the attack on Pinarcik, however, Mardin probably had been the least troubled of these three provinces.[34] This was because much of it is undulating farm and grazing land that is not particularly mountainous. Thus natural hiding places for the guerrillas were more difficult to find. In addition Pinarcik was not easily accessible from the Iraqi border, lying at least one day's walk away. Given these facts, the Turkish army's inability to determine where the PKK guerrillas who attacked Pinarcik had come from or fled to probably indicates the guerrillas' increasing effectiveness.

*Response.*--By its own admission, the response of the Turkish government to this escalation in PKK activity has been less than satisfactory. At the southern edge of Mardin, for example, the border with Syria had double, triple, and even quadruple lines of barbed-wire fencing. Manned watchtowers supposedly stood at approximately 200-meter intervals. Since these deterrents had not worked, however, new guard posts and fences, special spot-lights, and a sand which leaves foot traces of trespassers, were added along the 16-kilometer border line at Nusaybin by 1989. The 192-kilometer line from Nusaybin to the eastern Hamam area also has been fenced and new guard posts and spot-lights constructed. In addition a patrol road has been built and spot-lights are being added along the 26-kilometer border line with Syria from Nusaybin to the western Gulunce military station.[35]

Further east, near the Turkish-Iranian-Iraqi border convergence
in Hakkari province, the mountainous terrain becomes much rougher
and thus cannot be fenced. Army patrols and natural cliffs act as the
barriers. Turkish soldiers stop and frisk bus and automobile passen-
gers, as well as herdsmen at frequent checkpoints. A Turkish report
acknowledged, however, that: "Most of the PKK forces situated in
northern Iraq can easily walk across the border, carry out their attacks
and move out without being spotted. The situation is at times similar
at the Iranian border as well. The presence of gendarmerie forces at
the border line has proved to be nearly useless."[36]

Intelligence gathering has been a major problem for the govern-
ment. "Reports prepared by local officials as to the 'weakness' of
PKK forces," official sources now admit, "hardly reflect the truth."[37]
Usually a taboo subject, the MIT or Turkey's National Intelligence
Agency itself has even come under criticism.[38] The matter of the size
of the PKK's forces is a case in point.

Shortly after the attack on Pinarcik on June 20, 1987, Turkish
sources stated that "the Turkish intelligence believes that the PKK
guerrillas hiding inside the Turkish territory number no more than
300."[39] Less than a month later, however, the Turkish Prime Minister
himself, while visiting Mardin, declared that "there were exactly 3449
terrorists inside Turkey who were waging this undeclared war."[40] A
week later the same source that had reported Ozal's earlier remarks
now opined that "half of these had been caught or killed thus leaving
about 15 hundred left."[41]

At the same time, Sami (Sam) Cohen, a respected Turkish
journalist, wrote that "according to the Turkish government, the PKK
has some 1,100 armed men carrying out operations from within
Turkey, and a total estimated force of about 3,400 men."[42] Still
another report at that time stated that "the PKK is estimated to have
around 2,000 to 2,500 armed militants--about the same size as the
Provisional IRA," but added it hoped "to double the number of
militants by mid-1988."[43] By mid-1989, a new report asserted that the
PKK now "has an estimated 5,000 members."[44]

This confusion about the PKK was further reflected in the analysis
of "three separate pictures" drawn by "correspondents on the scene."[45]
The first, said to be "a well-known view frequently supported by
President Kenan Evren" was "that separatists well armed and traveling
in groups cross the borders of neighboring countries and enter Turkey
to carry out their attacks." The second was that "the PKK's so-called

forces reside in caves in the rugged region." Finally the third argued that "the PKK's militants are actually residents of villages in the same region and receive support from a handful of militants on the mountains who themselves receive their orders through couriers who cross the border with legal passports."

A Turkish colonel supported this third view by stating that: "They [the PKK] sit at the coffeehouse during the day. At night they dig up their guns and attack. When we arrive at the same coffeehouse they embrace us and tell us that we are their saviours." Prime Minister Turgut Ozal also reportedly believed in this third interpretation and even "went to the extent of accusing the people of Pinarcik . . . [of] cooperating with terrorists."

Given the inability of the Turkish military to protect every small village in the rough terrain of southeastern Turkey, as mentioned above, villagers loyal to the regime have been armed in an attempt to ward off PKK attacks. By March 1987, there were some 6,000 such village guards in place with at least two or three to a village.[46] Kenan Nehrozoglu, a member of the Turkish parliament from Mardin, however, argued that this was inherently the wrong approach: "They [the village guards] are a problem to the villagers; with their guns, rifles and pistols, they use force against their enemies in the villages."[47]

What is more these village guards and their families simply began to draw PKK fire and get themselves killed. As the government itself pointed out: "In a way, what has happened is that the state has singled out its supporters in rural settlements making them an easy target and identifying them for the terrorists."[48] Explaining why he had "resigned" from the local militia, one ex-guard stated: "After they started to shoot the families of village guards, I left my weapon and became one of the peasants again."[49] "Under these circumstances," admitted Turkish sources, "there is no way to defend the village guard system. . . . Whoever had the initial idea of arming the local populace there apparently failed to see its long-term impact."[50]

In addition Turkish sources tacitly have acknowledged some degree of popular support for the PKK: "Ankara must realize that these people are not defending their villages against a foreign enemy. Those who attack them [the villagers] are in any event closer to the people of that region because they use the local language and follow the local tradition and customs."[51] Elaborating, the same sources also have conceded that: "While most of the villagers do not trust gendarmerie forces, the latter do not trust them either."[52] Indeed, "according to regional sources who are well informed, one of the main routes of supplies to the PKK is the villages at the Iraqi border. Not only do they supply food and water but daily newspapers and magazines as well to the separatists."[53]

Although the guerrillas have struck hard at the village guards, Turkish sources also have pointed out that "the PKK is careful to make impressive gestures towards settlements which help them."[54] No doctors, for example, live in some isolated areas. To alleviate the problem "the PKK . . . bring in a doctor and look after the villagers-- at times giving them medicine for free. . . . The result in villages of this sort," admitted these sources, "can be nothing but sympathy."[55]

Poor communications also hamper the government in its efforts to respond. To reach the village where ten people had been killed by the PKK, for example, "Interior Minister Akbulut had to travel six hours by car to cover only 50 kilometers. The reason for this . . . [was] the terrible situation of mud-stricken roads."[56] Radio communication is often poor between a village and military base "because messages they [villagers under PKK attack] send can only travel about 2 km in the mountains as there is no antenna to relay them to 'base.'"[57] The same source added that the "massacre at Pinarcik, which has no wireless or telephone, highlighted the difficulty villagers have in calling for help when attacked."[58]

Even the Turkish military seems to suffer from equipment problems. A Turkish source, for example, reported how border guards at night "have no night binoculars. . . . How can we spot a movement when even in the moonlight we can see not more than about 20 meters,"[59] asked one soldier? "The most shocking part," of this equipment failure declared the same source, "was to see a petty officer with Turkish-made sports shoes . . . because the military boots-- apparently not intended to be used in the rugged territory--fell apart in not more than a month."

To effect a more efficient military response, "one of the highest level officials in Mardin said . . . against bandits, we need bandits. The new security forces should be trained like guerrillas, should live and fight like guerrillas. Stay on the mountains for months if necessary."[60] Increasing the military response, however, acknowledged other Turkish sources, would "alienate the people in the long run. . . . Even if we crush those on the mountains, new ones will go up in the future."[61] As another Turkish source concluded: "It is [a] general belief that a major scheme to improve living standards in the country's eastern parts . . . may be the only solid way to stop separatist violence."[62] Similarly a high level commander in the Uludere region stated that the military response was "no long-term solution. What we need is infrastructure, things that will make the people realize that they are one of us. New investments and new jobs."[63]

During the summer of 1987, martial law was lifted in the last four of Turkey's southeastern provinces that still had it dating from the late 1970s, and the position of Regional (Supra) Governor for the overall eight- (later eleven-) province area was created in Diyarbakir. Hayri Kozakcioglu, who already had been the provincial governor in Diyarbakir and was a former MIT official, was named to this new post and given very broad authority. Some of his most important powers included: (1) command over the special and general security forces; (2) control over the MIT as detailed by a special decree; (3) authorization to move around public employees and raise their salaries from 10 to 25 percent; (4) power to evacuate or merge villages and pasture areas; (5) supervision over civil trial procedures carried out against security forces; and (6) authority to order provincial governors to take "necessary measures."[64] With justification some observers termed this new situation "civilian martial law."[65]

By the fall of 1989, however, it was clear that the various state security forces--which included the army, army intelligence, gendarmerie, gendarmerie intelligence gathering operation, political police, police intelligence, special police squads, MIT, Directorate for Counter-Terrorism and Operations (TMHDB), and village guards-- lacked the necessary coordination. The office of the Supra Governor had been unable to control, much less solve, the escalating problem. As one report put it: "A number of departments are functioning in the troubled region but there is an obvious vacuum of authority . . . . PKK units . . . are roaming the region receiving logistic support from the locals."[66] Some of Kozakcioglu's power was transferred directly to the army under the command of the Chief of Staff in Ankara, General Necip Torumtay, who declared that "conditions of War . . . exist[ed] in southeast Turkey."[67]

*Problems.*--Despite its apparent achievement in the field during 1987, the PKK suffered a serious setback at the end of the year when its alliance with Barzani's KDP was terminated. Indeed relations between the two had been cooling since 1985 because of the PKK's violent tactics against women and children and even members of the

KDP itself. In May 1987, the KDP issued a warning to the PKK as required under the "Principles of Solidarity" they had signed in 1983. In this warning the KDP declared that "it is clear they [the PKK] have adopted an aggressive attitude towards the leadership of our party, towards its policies and the friends of our party." Continuing Barzani's party denounced what it termed "terrorist operations within the country and abroad and their actions to liquidate human beings. . . . The mentality behind such action is against humanity and democracy and is not in line with the national liberation of Kurdistan."[68]

Ironically 1988 witnessed the KDP appealing successfully to Turkey for refuge when, with the end of the Gulf War, Iraq was able to defeat Barzani's Kurds. Some 60,000 Iraqi Kurds were allowed to enter southeastern Turkey in what Ankara billed as a humanitarian gesture.[69] Others, however, argued that Turkey's real motive was to be able to keep a closer watch on the KDP or even control its own Kurds better by setting the Iraqi Kurds against them in a contest for the land.[70]

Conscious of its need for new allies, the PKK issued a call to all Turkish Kurds for *havakiri* (action unity). The SPTK, *Rizgari*, and Kawa, however, rejected the offer because of Ocalan's violent tactics against civilians and, along with at least five other Turkish Kurdish organizations--including the KUK, *Ala Rizgari*, the PPKK and the socialist wing of the KUK (KUK-SE)--established an alliance against the PKK called Tevger or the Kurdistan Liberation Movement. The SPTK leader, Kemal Burkay, was named the head of this new grouping.

Although the program of Tevger called for the establishment of an independent Kurdish state, it did not approve of terrorism. Copies of Tevger's program were reportedly seized by the police in Diyarbakir province in August 1988.[71] It is difficult, however, to envision the new grouping exercising much direct pressure in southeastern Turkey against the PKK since most of its members are based in Europe.

Potentially more ominous for the PKK was the possibility that it might soon have to face opposition from other armed, radical leftist organizations in Turkey. Dev Yol, the Turkish Workers-Peasants Liberation Army (TIKKO), and the Road of the Turkish Revolution (TDY) supposedly agreed to fight the PKK on its own grounds if it continued to attack civilians. This decision was reportedly taken in Paris during the winter of 1987-88 and then approved at a meeting held in Munich. The PKK was termed a "fascist" organization because of its tactics and its "minimum target" of establishing a "Kurdish state."[72]

What is more recent defections from the PKK have added to its problems. Huseyin Yildirim, a Kurdish lawyer living in Sweden and for several years the spokesman for the PKK in Europe, became disgruntled over the party's policy of killing civilians and contemplated the creation of a less violent "Kurdish Revolutionary Workers Party" as a rival to the PKK.[73] Following a sympathetic interview with Ocalan published in the Turkish newspaper *Milliyet* in June 1988 (see below) on the other hand, Yildirim denounced Ocalan for sending "a message of submission and concession to the Turkish state" and claimed that Ocalan had "sold out his party." More to the point, Yildirim declared that "after the party is relieved from Apo, the armed struggle will start again. But this time women and children will not be selected as targets."[74]

After the two PKK leaders exchanged accusations that the other was collaborating with Turkey,[75] four messengers from Yildirim to Ocalan in Syria were apparently killed. Ocalan incredulously claimed that they had "committed suicide. They had bad intentions."[76] In a speech at the Mahsun Korkmaz Military Academy, Ocalan accused Yildirim of being "an agent for European imperialism" which was trying to pacify the PKK so that the borders of Turkey, a NATO member, would not be endangered.

> Their intention is to corrupt the PKK. They will first corrupt the ideological-political-military structure and then turn the PKK into a tool for their imperialist aims in the region just like other organizations.[77]

As for calls for a "Democratic PKK," Ocalan declared that there would be no concessions, listing as an example the initial creation of the Communist Party of the Soviet Union and the case of Rosa Luxembourg. "We believe that today in Kurdistan, the movement should be based on discipline . . . and central control."[78]

As mentioned in Chapter 5, Ocalan's former wife, Kesire Yildirim, who for many years was one of his closest associates, has also broken away from the organization. After being placed under "house arrest," she finally managed to escape and is now siding with Huseyin Yildirim (not a relative) in an effort to build a new party abroad.[79]

In addition a number of other prominent members of the PKK have abandoned it either after being apprehended or giving themselves up to the police. In return for information on the PKK these militants have been granted lesser punishments under a so-called "Repentants' Law." Sometimes these repentants are even given a change of identity to protect them from PKK retribution. (A number of these "confessions, however, have proven false either out of a desire to blame others, avoid prison, or purposely sow seeds of confusion.)

On January 18, 1989, Halit (Hayri) Celik, a PKK regional leader in the Garzan area (which includes Sasan, Bismil, Silvan, Kozluk, Sirvan, Siirt, Kurtalan, Batman, Besire, Baykan, Bitlis, and Tatvan) was captured by Turkish security forces. Recep (Ferhat) Tiril, another regional leader in Garzan, surrendered on the same day. A month later Mehmet Emin Karatay, the PKK regional leader in the province of Mardin, was captured. Based on subsequent events, however, the Turkish claim that "as a result of these three incidents . . . a major proportion of the PKK leadership has been crushed and currently militants in the region have been left without leaders," rings false.[79]

Finally speculation has arisen concerning a possible PKK-Idealist confrontation. In November 1988, a former member of Alparslan Turkes' fascist NAP, reincarnated after the 1980 coup as the Nationalist Labour Party, was killed by the PKK shortly after he was freed from prison despite four death sentences for murders of left-wing militants.[80] Commenting on the situation, an important Idealist ideologist declared:

> They [the Turkish state] are trying to bring us face to face with the PKK. They are trying to use us to combat the PKK just like the situation before the 1980 takeover. We will not become the pawns once again. Battling separatism is a national duty but first of all, a duty of the state.[81]

*New support.*--Despite these setbacks, invaluable Syrian support for the PKK continued. (See below in Chapter 7.) In addition the KUK and possibly Kawa too have indicated their willingness to join the PKK in its guerrilla warfare if the latter were willing to change its tactics.[82] (The practical support either one of these two Turkish Kurdish groups could bring, however, would seem very limited.)

Key to its new found support and success has been the decision by the PKK to abandon its blatantly terrorist policy of killing women and children in favor of one stressing assaults on economic targets such as bridges, roads, rail links, and industrial plants.[83] Furthermore the PKK incredulously began to claim that the civilian killings that had occurred were really the work of the MIT who then tried to put the blame on it. Somewhat illogically, therefore, the PKK also argued that, even if some civilians had been killed, they deserved to be since they were relatives of state collaborators: "The allegations of the Turkish rulers that the liberation movement attacked also civilians is a shameless lie. The so-called 'civilians' are well-armed and well-paid mercenaries who bring dishonor to the name 'Kurd.'"[84] In any case it was clear that by 1989 the PKK had decided to stop attacking civilian targets.

A potentially important ally was gained when Dev Sol (Revolutionary Left), known before the coup in 1980 for its violent activities in cities and among students, became the first member of the Turkish radical left to break ranks on the issue and signed a protocol "to cooperate with and support the PKK both in Turkey and abroad."[85] Reportedly Ocalan met in person with the Dev Sol leaders to negotiate the understanding. A spokesman for the radical left organization declared: "We now accept that the PKK is waging a legitimate war and although we do not approve of all of their activities, [a reference to the killing of civilians] we must understand that in their territory, they have no other alternative."

An operational alliance between the PKK and Dev Sol would offer each new opportunities as each would be able to add a dimension to its capacity that was previously lacking. Dev Sol would be able to send some of its members to rural areas either for training or to be hidden, while the PKK would be able to obtain safe houses and other facilities in the urban areas.

By the summer of 1989, the PKK had gained at least two other allies from the radical Turkish left: (1)the Acilciler faction of the Turkish Peoples Liberation Party and Front (THKP-C) and (2)the Turkish Communist Party-Marxist Leninist organization (TKP-ML), which is the political front of the violent Turkish Workers-Peasants Liberation Army (TIKKO).[86] Mihrac Ural, the leader of Acilciler, declared that he and Ocalan were "the closest of friends" and that he would be sending his militants, based in the Bekaa Valley of Lebanon and believed to number less than fifty, to train at PKK bases. Ural himself, however, continues to live in Paris and possesses Syrian citizenship.

In a communique issued in West Germany the TKP-ML stated that it accepted the PKK as a "national movement" and called Turkey "an enemy." Since the TKP-ML apparently has a strong structure in a number of Turkish cities, especially Istanbul, the PKK is now in an even better position to obtain safe houses in urban areas.

Finally Celal Talabani, the Iraqi Kurdish leader of the Patriotic Union of Kurdistan (PUK), also has begun to support the PKK. On May 1, 1988, he signed a "Protocol of Understanding" with Ocalan in Damascus[87] and threatened to give overt support to him if Turkey again entered northern Iraq.[88] Since the PUK was almost equal to the KDP in the number of fighters it possessed, Talabani's declaration potentially offered the PKK a substitute for the lost KDP alliance. Accordingly the Iraqi government's rout of its rebellious Kurds following the end of the Gulf War, also struck a blow at the PKK.

*Apo's Milliyet interview.*--In June 1988, the independent Turkish newspaper *Milliyet* published for two days a very sympathetic interview the well-known Turkish journalist Mehmet Ali Birand conducted with Abdullah Ocalan.[89]   Photographs of the insurgent leader at the Mahsun Korkmaz Military Academy, complete with his armed militants in the background, were included.  Ocalan was quoted as seeking to establish a dialogue with Turkey.  Incredulously he claimed that he "hated weapons" and had never touched a gun in his life. Rather the PKK leader stated that he loved to watch football games and was a strong fan of the Turkish Galatasaray team.

"I love birds," and "am against the killing of [the] innocent," Ocalan added.  When he first had come to Ankara and seen the statue of modern Turkey's founder, Ataturk, he had been very excited. The massacres committed by the PKK were "an organizational mistake."

To demonstrate that he was not serving as a mere conduit for PKK propaganda, Birand prefixed the interview with a statement that he had no intention to serve the purposes of the PKK, "was proud to be a Turk," and opposed the massacres that had occurred.  It was simply his journalistic duty to publish what Ocalan had said without editorial comment.

As mentioned above in Chapter 4, the Turkish government banned further publication of the interview after its second day in print, claiming that it was "showing the PKK as if it was in the defence of a legal right" and "disassociating" it from what it really was. Since this would weaken national unity, Article 142/3 of the Turkish Penal Code had been violated. Birand was acquitted of the charges the following year.

*Renewed offenses.*--Although attempts by the PKK to hold a "spring congress" in Turkish territory during 1988 and 1989 failed, it was becoming clear "that the balance in southeast Turkey was gradually shifting to the benefit of the PKK."[90] Despite the checkered record of the PKK, Turkish sources confessed that "a survey conducted in the troubled region earlier this month [February 1989] has concluded that the amount of support enjoyed by the separatists has increased since last year" and that "the situation in the southeast is deteriorating."[91]

According to "one reliable [PKK] source," the PKK had "lived through a major change in strategy after . . . last year." Ocalan now realized that civilian massacres were self-defeating. "The mistakes of the past have been overcome. The PKK is now accepted, against all of these mistakes, as the only organization in the region which has raised the flag of resistance."[92] No longer were the local people referring to the PKK as the *talebes* (students) or the *eshkiyas* (bandits). Rather the term *Cephe* (Front, short for the ERNK) had come into use. One Turkish source even stated that: "Many people, clearly affiliated with the Front, believe that terror in that region is not initiated by the separatists but by Turkey's forces combating terrorism."

Illustrative of the PKK's new strategy, was its attack on the Sirnak Coal Mine in Siirt province in May 1989. Until the Turkish military had taken over direct responsibility for the area, the government had allowed the local population to carry off coal from the mine at night. Now, however, such activities were being punished by beatings and the destruction of the donkeys used to haul the fuel away.

The PKK struck when many villagers were at the mine. The party delivered a propaganda speech and supposedly "kidnapped" twenty youngsters as recruits. (It was more likely that the recruiting was accomplished voluntarily.) None of the villagers were killed. As the PKK departed, they destroyed several automobiles owned by the coal company. The attack was a successful, symbolic assertion of the claim by the PKK that it was serving the needs of the local population, while the Turkish state was a cruel occupier.

Turkish forces struck back almost immediately against PKK militants near the Demiraya and Baglica villages on Seyh Omer mountain. The retaliation led to the death of twelve guerrillas, including three of their regional leaders, and a Syrian who apparently had been recruited in the Syrian-controlled Bekaa Valley. The three dead PKK leaders were Halit (Fadil) Igneli, Ramazan (Sait) Tavsan, and Emin (Eyup) Polat. They had supposedly been responsible for the deaths of at least seventy civilians and eleven security officials.

By September 1989, more than 1500 people had died since the PKK had begun its campaign in August 1984.[93] Abdulkadir Aksu, the newly appointed Minister of the Interior, warned that this death toll was "rising steadily."[94] The Regional Governor, Hayri Kozakcioglu, revealed that during the first six months of 1989, there had been a total of 258 PKK-related incidents, compared to only 315 for the entire year of 1988.[95] The PKK had even established at least two mobile, clandestine radio stations.

In late August heavy fighting occurred in the Cudi mountains just north of the Iraqi border near Sirnak township in the province of Siirt. A major government push to eliminate the guerrillas came up empty handed, however, when the PKK simply melted away. Amidst an apparent vacuum of civilian authority, the Chief of Staff in Ankara, General Necip Torumtay, issued a tough written statement: "There is no other alternative but to accept those who use weapons against national existence and sovereignty and those who willingly and knowingly support them, as enemies and take measures accordingly. . . . We have to use guns against guns quite apart from our long term propositions and projects."[96]

Torumtay's statement was widely believed to mean that the Turks would begin emphasizing sticks instead of carrots in dealing with the problem. In effect undeclared martial law would be instituted under the office of the Regional Governor. Under the circumstances such an approach was understandable, but only on a short-term basis. As Erdal Inonu, the leader of the main opposition party SHP noted: "What matters is to remember that creating gaps between [the] security forces and the people is the target of this struggle and to evaluate things in this way."[97]

During the spring of 1990, the situation continued to escalate as incidents started to occur in urban areas.[98] In what some Kurds began to call the "Kurdish intifadah," teenagers for the first time started to throw stones at the security forces, erect roadblocks, and burn tires in the provinces of Mardin, Siirt, and Elazig. Certain shops, offices, and schools were closed to protest what some referred to as "the brutal action of the security forces."

On March 23, 1990, thousands of people marched through the streets of Cizre in the province of Mardin shouting "Down with Turkey" and "Long live free Kurdistan." A Turkish intelligence report stated that the PKK was now operating in major cities, encouraging popular opposition to the state, and urging organized demonstrations, strikes, boycotts, and seizures of public buildings. A senior government official declared: "This is beginning to turn into a new and different situation." He added that "we are sure most people still do not want to get involved, but they are either forced by the PKK or carried away by this new hysteria." At any rate it was clear that the PKK had managed to escalate its campaign against the Turkish government to a new and higher level of intensity.

## Notes

1. *Briefing Study*. See note 3 in Chapter 5 for a full description of this source.

2. Martin van Bruinessen, "Between Guerrilla War and Political Murder: The Workers' Party of Kurdistan," *Middle East Report*, No. 153 (July-Aug. 1988), p. 44.

3. *Ibid.*

4. The following discussion is based on "Serious Measures Called for in New 'Attack Season,'" *Briefing*, Feb. 27, 1989, p. 17.

5. Sam Cohen, "Turkey's Mysterious Strike in Iraq Underlines Ongoing Effort to Uproot Kurdish Nationalism," *Christian Science Monitor*, July 14, 1983, p. 12. Also see G. H. Jansen, "The Turks Join In," *Middle East International*, June 10, 1983; and "Turkey's Move against the Kurds," *Mid East Markets*, June 13, 1983.

6. Martin van Bruinessen, "The Kurds between Iran and Iraq," *Middle East Report*, No. 141 (July-Aug. 1986), p. 27n15.

7. See "The Common Enemy," *The Economist*, June 18, 1983, pp. 55-56. Also see "Turkey, Iraq Agree on Hunting Kurds," *Monday Morning*, June 6, 1983.

8. Bruinessen, "Kurds between Iran and Iraq," p. 26.

9. *Briefing Study*.

10. *Ibid.*

11. "Turkish Troops Step Up Anti-Kurdish Campaign," *Arab News*, Mar. 21, 1988.

12. "F. Almanya'da PKK'ya Darbe," *Milliyet*, Jan. 2, 1989.

13. "Terrorist Attacks in Eastern Turkey," *Briefing*, Oct. 15, 1984, pp. 11-12; and "The Pawns in the Game of International Terrorism," *Briefing*, Oct. 29, 1984. See also the reports in Artun Unsal, "L'armee pourrait effectuer une nouvelle operation contre les maquisards Kurdes en territoire irakien," *Le Monde*, Oct. 17, 1984; Michel Dubuisson, "Les Turcs authorises a penetrer en Irak (et en Iran?) pour chasser les Kurdes," *Le Soir*, Oct. 19, 1984; and "La Turquie va 'ratisser' les Kurdes en Irak," *Le Matin*, Oct. 18, 1984.

14. See "17 Terrorists Caught in Southeast Turkey," *Turkish Daily News* (International Edition), Nov. 30-Dec. 6, 1984, p. 3.

15. Cited in *Briefing Study*.

16. *Ibid.*

17. *Ibid.*

18. "PKK's Spring Offensive: An Act of Desperation," *Briefing*, May 16-23, 1988, p. 10.

19. "Kurds Killed in Turkish Air Raid on Guerrilla Hide-outs in Iraq," *Financial Times*, Aug. 21, 1986.

20. "Turks Said Showing New Resolve to Put Down Rebellion by Kurdish Separatists; Kurds Strike," *The Armenian Reporter*, Sept. 11, 1986, p. 1. Also see the reports in "Turks Bomb Kurdish Rebel Camp," *The Armenian Weekly*, Aug. 30, 1986, p. 3; "Kurdish Leader [Barzani] Issues Threats at Turks Following Raid," in *ibid.*; and "Turquie: Un raid contre les rebelles Kurdes en Irak aurait fait entre 150 et 200 morts," *Le Monde*, Aug. 23, 1986.

21. Cited in *Briefing Study*.

22. *Ibid.*

23. Bruinessen, "Workers' Party of Kurdistan," p. 46.

24. "Turkish Air Force Jets Bomb Kurdish Camps in Northern Iraq," *The Armenian Reporter*, Mar. 5, 1987, pp. 1, 14. Also see "Turkish Warplanes Raid Kurdish Guerrilla Bases in Iraq," *The Armenian Mirror-Spectator*, Mar. 14, 1987, pp. 1, 3.

25. *Briefing*, May 16-23, 1988, p. 10.

26. "Terror in the East--The Massacre and the PKK," *Briefing*, June 29, 1987, p. 9.

27. "The PKK Challenge: What [Is] the Next Step?" *Briefing*, July 13, 1987, pp. 3, 4.

28. "PKK Strikes Again: The Attacks Will Continue," *Briefing*, Aug. 24, 1987, p. 13.

29. *Ibid.*, pp. 13-14. See also "How the Kurds Shook the West," *The Economist*, June 27, 1987, pp. 49-50, for a rather detailed report which tends to vindicate this assessment of the PKK's accomplishment.

30. For a listing of most of these "lesser attacks," see, under the incongruous title, "PKK in Action: It Is Getting Weaker!" *Briefing*, July 20, 1987, pp. 8-9.

31. "PKK Survey: Impact of Rural Violence," *Briefing*, Aug. 17, 1987, p. 6.

32. *Briefing*, July 13, 1987, p. 5.

33. *Briefing*, June 29, 1987, p. 11.

34. The following discussion is based on *The Economist*, June 27, 1987, pp. 49-50; *Briefing*, July 13, 1987, p. 3; and *ibid.*, Aug. 24, 1987, pp. 13, 14.

35. "Combatting Terrorism: Death Toll 396," *Briefing*, Jan. 16, 1989, p. 14.

36. "PKK Survey-IV: Countering Psychological Warfare," *Briefing*, Sept. 7, 1987, p. 12.

37. *Briefing*, Aug. 24, 1987, p. 13.

38. See, for example, "The Strange Case of Hurriyet Photos," *Briefing*, July 27, 1987, pp. 3-6; and the discussion of "MIT Under Fire" in the same issue.

39. *Briefing*, June 29, 1987, p. 11.

40. *Briefing*, July 13, 1987, p. 3.

41. *Briefing*, July 20, 1987, p. 10.

42. Sam Cohen, "Turkey Pursues Two-track Policy to Stem Kurdish Violence," *Christian Science Monitor*, July 27, 1987, p. 11.

43. "Turkey's Kurds and the Gulf War," *Mid East Markets*, Jan. 25, 1988.

44. Aliza Marcus, "Battle for Control of a Province," *Christian Science Monitor*, Aug. 25, 1989, p. 6.

45. The following discussion and citations are drawn from "The PKK Threat: A Myth or a Reality," *Briefing*, July 20, 1987, p. 10.

46. "A Remote but Bitter War: Kurds and Turks Fight It Out in the 'Wild East,'"*Newsweek*, Mar. 30, 1987, p. 45.

47. Cited in U.S. Helsinki Watch Committee, *Destroying Ethnic Identity: The Kurds of Turkey* (New York and Washington: U.S. Helsinki Watch Committee, 1988), p. 26.

48. "PKK Survey-II: Security Crisis in the Troubled Region," *Briefing*, Aug. 24, 1987, p. 11.

49. *Briefing*, Aug. 17, 1987, p. 7.

50. *Briefing*, Aug. 24, 1987, p. 11.

51. *Ibid.*

52. *Ibid.*, p. 13.

53. *Briefing*, Aug. 17, 1987, p. 8.

54. *Ibid.*

55. *Ibid.*, pp. 8-9.

56. *Briefing*, Feb. 2, 1987, p. 11.

57. *Briefing*, Aug. 24, 1987, p. 15.

58. *Briefing*, July 13, 1987, p. 3.

59. This and the following citation were taken from *Briefing.*, Aug. 24, 1987, p. 16.

60. Cited in *ibid.*

61. *Ibid.*

62. *Briefing*, Feb. 2, 1987, p. 11.

63. *Briefing.*, Aug. 24, 1987, p. 16.

64. See "The Powers of the Supra Governor," *Briefing*, July 20, 1987, p. 12.

65. *Briefing*, July 20, 1987, p. 9.

66. "A More Realistic Approach in the Offing?" *Briefing*, Aug. 28, 1989, pp. 16, 13.

67. "Southeast Security: Further Measures Called for," *Briefing*, Sept. 11, 1989, p. 17.

68. Cited in *Briefing Study*.

69. Sam Cohen, "Turkey Anxious About Presence of Iraqi Kurds," *Christian Science Monitor*, Sept. 12, 1988, p. 4.

70. Garen Yegparian, "Defeat of the Iraqi-Kurdish Movement: Lessons To Be Learned," *The Armenian Weekly*, Sept. 17, 1988, pp. 2, 3.

71. *Cumhuriyet*, Aug. 25, 1988.

72. *Briefing Study*.

73. "Will the PKK Be a Regional Issue?" *Briefing*, Mar. 14, 1988, p. 11.

74. "PKK: The European Breakup," *Briefing*, Sept. 5, 1988, p. 11.

75. *Milliyet*, Sept. 13, 1988.

76. Cited in "Serious Measures Called for in New 'Attack Season,'" *Briefing*, Feb. 27, 1989, p. 11.

77. Cited in "Yildirim, An Agent of Europe?" *Briefing*, Mar. 27, 1989, p. 20.

78. Cited in *ibid.*

79. "Three Heavy Blows to PKK," *Briefing*, Apr. 17, 1989, p. 10.

80. *Tercuman*, Nov. 2, 1988.

81. Cited in "Security Crisis Overcome but Upsurge in Terrorism," *Briefing*, Jan. 2, 1989, p. 20.

82. *Briefing Study*.

83. See "Turkey's Kurds and the Gulf War," *Mid East Markets*, Jan., 25, 1989.

84. National Liberation Front of Kurdistan [PKK], "Genocide: After the Armenians, the Kurds", July 1987, p. 27.

85. This and the following citation were taken from "DEV-SOL/PKK Sign 'Blood Pact,'" *Briefing*, Aug. 22, 1988, pp. 14-16.

86. See Chapter 2 and 3 above on these two groups before 1980. The following discussion is based on "The PKK: Botan Group at Verge of Destruction but Final Solution Still Far Away," *Briefing*, Aug. 14, 1989, p. 19.

87. "A Good-Will Gesture: But at What Cost?" *Briefing*, Sept. 12, 1988, p. 6.

88. *Briefing*, Mar. 14, 1988, p. 8.

89. The following information is taken from "The Case of the 'Apo' Interview," *Briefing*, June 20, 1988, pp. 17-18.

90. *Briefing*, Aug. 14, 1989, p. 14.

91. *Briefing*, Feb. 27, 1989, p. 14.

92. This citation and the following data are taken from *ibid.*, pp. 15-16.

93. Marcus, "Battle for a Province," p. 6.

94. *Turkey Briefing*, July 1989.

95. Marcus, "Battle for a Province," p. 6.

96. Cited in "Torumtay Statement Welcomed but What About the Government?" *Briefing*, Aug. 21, 1989, p. 13.

97. Cited in *Briefing*, Aug. 14, 1989, p. 15.

98. The following analysis and citations were taken from Sam Cohen, "Turks Seek to Limit New Phase of Kurdish Rebellion," *Christian Science Monitor*, Mar. 27, 1990, p. 4.

# 7

---

# Transnational Influences

Many Turks, and their government, feel that the PKK and other Kurdish separatists have been receiving aid from various states and groups which desire a weakened Turkey. The President of Turkey himself, Kenan Evren, was reported to have declared in October 1981, for example, that the Kurdish problem stems from foreign incitement.[1] Ilhan Cevik, the chairman and founder of the *Turkish Daily News*, wrote in November 1985 that: "It is a historical fact that there are ethnic groups in the Iraqi and Syrian border areas which have been variously exploited, supported materially and morally, and provoked by foreign powers."[2] In his "Statement" of August 1989 on the escalating PKK guerrilla operations, General Necip Torumtay, the Chief of Staff in Ankara, asserted "that the PKK ... receives important support from foreign powers."[3] Commenting on Torumtay's "Statement," a knowledgeable Turkish source concluded: "As long as separatist camps remain open in Syria, Lebanon, Iran and Iraq, and as long as they receive indirect support from European countries, Turkey will have to counter a resurrection of armed terrorism every year."[4]

In taking this position the Turks undoubtedly have been influenced by their historical memories of European imperialist schemes to weaken and divide the Ottoman Empire in the nineteenth and early twentieth centuries. Even after the establishment of the Turkish Republic in the 1920s, the Turks suspected that the British had backed Sheikh Said's Kurdish revolt in eastern Turkey during 1925 to weaken the Turkish claim to Mosul which was largely inhabited by Kurds. A Kurdish revolt against Turkey would vitiate Turkey's claim that it would best represent the Kurds of Mosul.

The Turks, however, were not able to produce any serious evidence to substantiate their suspicions. On the other hand the Kurdish revolt was crushed in part because the French gave the Turks permission to use the Baghdad railroad that passed through Syria for troop transport.[5] Similarly during the Kurdish revolt around Mt. Ararat in 1930, although the Kurds did receive some help from the Armenians (see below), Iran allowed Turkish troops to pass through its territory and surround the insurgents. Iran and Turkey later legalized their agreement by making minor border adjustments in 1932.[6] In addition under the Treaty of Saadabad in 1937 and the Baghdad Pact of 1955, Turkey, Iran, and Iraq all agreed, in part, to cooperate on the Kurdish question.[7] This collaboration included measures to prevent cross-border communication and support among the Kurds and, in general, sought to prevent any joint, transnational Kurdish action that might challenge the present international boundaries. The purpose of this chapter is specifically to analyze the transnational influences that exist on the contemporary Kurdish problem in Turkey.

## The Mideast

A recent commentary on the Kurdish problem in Turkey declared:

> Countries neighboring Turkey in the Middle East, Iran, Iraq and Syria, have been used for years by terrorists as secure grounds for training activities, arms supplies, cross-border attacks and establishing political or military headquarters.[8]

Turkish intelligence sources have charged that PKK bases have existed just across the border in all three of Turkey's southern neighbors. In Iran, these camps supposedly have been located at Selvana, Rezhan, and Ziveh; in Iraq, at Sinhat, Kishan, Nirve, Lolan, and Deryasor; and in Syria, at Kamisli and Resulyan.[9] A closer analysis of these three states indicates, however, that Syria has given the PKK by far the most overt support, while Iraq at least has made the most attempts to cooperate with the Turks, even giving Turkey carte blanche permission to pursue the PKK into northern Iraq on four different occasions since 1983. Iran's role in this matter has fallen somewhere in between these two extremes.

*Syria.*--As detailed above in Chapters 5 and 6, Syria has provided a haven for Abdullah (Apo) Ocalan, the leader of the PKK, since before the Turkish coup of 1980. After this event, the Syrians permitted the remnants of the PKK to reassemble and reconstitute themselves on their territory and in the parts of Lebanon they controlled. The first three PKK "congresses" also took place there. To this day, Ocalan continues to live in Damascus.

There are probably a number of reasons for this situation. Smoldering animosities concerning the Turkish annexation of Hatay (Alexandretta) province in 1939, as well as current problems dealing with the waters of the Euphrates River, which first flows through Turkey before reaching Syria, have long kept Turkish-Syrian relations cool. (When completed in the 1990s, Turkey's giant Ataturk Dam is projected to be able to divert half of the more than 26 trillion liters of water that flows into Syria.) In addition disagreements exist over Cyprus, Israel, and the PLO leadership. The memories of the harsh Ottoman rule that lasted into the early years of the twentieth century also probably play a background role. Finally one should mention the grandiose ambitions of Syria's leader, Hafez Assad, to occupy a dominant position in the region.

In July 1987, Turkish Prime Minister Turgut Ozal signed a security protocol with the Syrians in Damascus. Under its terms Syria agreed to stop permitting the PKK to raid Turkey from Syrian borders and to remove the PKK camps from its territory. For its part Ankara agreed to supply Syria with no less that 500 cubic meters per second of water per month. A request for the extradition of Ocalan, however, was refused.

Further Syrian intransigency soon became evident as the PKK camps were simply moved to the Syrian-controlled parts of the Bekaa Valley which were supposedly beyond Syrian legal control. "There is still evidence that Syrian territory is being used in many of the PKK attacks which are still taking place," concluded a Turkish report in July 1989.[10] Reportedly at another high level meeting between the two states in Mardin during June 1988, Syria again rejected a request for Ocalan's extradition, apparently wanting to keep him as a "trump card" for the future.[11] Another Turkish report sarcastically concluded that "the security protocol signed between the two countries [had] turned, in practice, into a disagreement agreement."[12]

*Iran.*--Given the profound ideological differences between secularized Turkey and Islamic Iran, the two states have been able to maintain surprisingly friendly relations. This is because both have calculated that such a policy would serve their respective interests.[13] As a result, Iran has never served the role of PKK safe house played for so long by Syria.

Nevertheless tensions exist. During the Gulf War, both Iran and Iraq armed the other side's Kurds as fifth-column allies. Thus Tehran supported the Iraqi Kurds who harbored the PKK. Turkish incursions against these Kurds in pursuit of the PKK inevitably drew Iranian disapproval. What is more Iran refused to allow the Turkish military to pursue the PKK across its borders as the Iraqis did. As one observer noted: "The Turks could reasonably complain to both Iran and Iraq that by arming the Kurds they risk[ed] destabilizing the whole Turkish-Iraq-Iran triangle."[14]

In the summer of 1989, a Turkish source charged that, in addition to the PKK camps that had been in Iran for sometime already, a new one had been established at Ucneviye north of Urumiye with support from the Eastern bloc and Cuba.[15] According to Fatih Tan, a PKK repentant, the PKK camps in Iran consisted of about twenty-five militants under the command of Ocalan's brother, Osman Ocalan. Supposedly some eighty PKK guerrillas had infiltrated into Turkey over the Iranian border in April 1989. Most of them had been trained at the Resistance Camp of Ahmet Kesip and the Orencik Martyrs.

Another report indicated that the two PKK mobile radio stations that had been established clandestinely were believed to be in Iran.[16] In addition further data indicated an "extensive PKK force deployment from camps in Iranian territory to the . . . buffer zone between Iran and Iraq."[17] Some 200 PKK guerrillas were now based at the Basiyan region where the borders of Turkey, Iran, and Iraq form an inverted triangle. They were "located in such a way that the terrorists may immediately pull back into Iran . . . preventing any cross-border attacks of Turkish troops."[18] Despite these problems, one Turkish study still concluded that "since November 1984 there have been only a few PKK attacks originating from Iran. . . . Tehran was generally careful to restrict the PKK's activities in Iran."[19]

*Iraq.*--As noted above, Iraq has permitted Turkey to pursue PKK guerrillas into its territory on four different occasions since 1983.

Thus, although Iraqi bases have been invaluable to the PKK, they were not enjoyed with the permission of the host government.

According to a recent Turkish report, now that the Gulf War is over and the Iraqi government has regained control of its northern (Kurdish) areas, PKK camps are still maintained there as well camouflaged "tent camps" in mountainous places which are very hard to reach. As of the summer of 1989, such camps were supposedly to be found in Kishan, Duruk, Urah, Gulkan, Besili, Sutuni, Zivek, Artis, Nazdur, Birri, Kiru, Barzan, Hayat, Ikmalah, S. Yunis, and Durjan.[20]

Despite its cooperation with Turkey, some Turkish officials have charged that Iraq discretely supplied weapons to the PKK in return for information about Massoud Barzani's Iraqi KDP. One Turkish officer declared: "The Iraqi regime has an interest in the border region where they cannot enter because of Barzani forces. They [Iraq] give weapons and ammunition to the PKK in order to receive information on activities of Iraqi Kurds. The PKK while on one hand receives support from those Kurds on the other sells them out for its own survival."[21]

Another report seconded this claim: "Baghdad is now reported supplying the PKK with guns and ammunition in exchange for information. The feeling is the PKK is telling Iraqi troops where Barzani's camps are."[22] If these reports of Iraqi duplicity are valid, they help explain why the Iraqi KDP broke its alliance with the PKK at the end of 1987.

*Gulf War.*--The Mosul-Kirkuk area in northern Iraq is inhabited by some 1,000,000 Iraqi Kurds who had become virtually autonomous given Iraq's desperate need to concentrate on its fight for survival against Iran during the Gulf War (1980-1988). The possibility that Turkey might try to occupy this oil-rich area in the aftermath of an Iraqi collapse contained immense international implications.[23] Indeed the Turks had only given up their claim to this region in 1925 after a protracted dispute with Britain, which held Iraq as a mandate from the League of Nations. Since then the Turks had viewed the Mosul-Kirkuk region as having been taken away from them at a moment of political weakness. Given Turkey's great need for oil, perceived interest in suppressing any possible Kurdish state that might be created in northern Iraq following an Iranian victory, and the PKK's longtime usage of northern Iraq as a sanctuary for raids into southeastern Turkey, Turkish military action seemed plausible.

Of immediate concern, however, was the strategic pipeline which carried a million barrels of oil a day from Kirkuk to Iskenderun in Turkey. This pipeline met one-third of Turkey's oil needs, and also provided some $300 million in Iraqi rental fees. The Turkish authorities warned Iran against striking it following threats by Khomeini's government to do just that in its attempt to launch an offensive into northern Iraq. Iran's refusal to guarantee the integrity of the pipeline was described by a Turkish official as "unfortunate" because his country could not remain a spectator if its "crucial interests" were harmed.

In August 1987, Turkish border officials in Hakkari province intercepted a special operations company of the Iranian Revolutionary Guards Corps near Semdinli and took into custody ninety-five prisoners. Turkish officials claimed that the Iranians were trying to sabotage the pipeline, but the Iranians protested they were merely trying to attack a hostile Kurdish guerrilla camp in northern Iraq. After diplomatic discussions the Turks repatriated the prisoners.

Thus the pipeline issue led to speculation in the Turkish press concerning a possible Turkish military operation to save it from Iranian forces and their Iraqi Kurdish allies, Barzani's KDP, which, as pointed out above in Chapter 6, supported the PKK. Turkish military sources stated privately they were studying possible options, including the military one.

Huseyin Avni Guler, a former Turkish intelligence officer, and Hasan Isik, a former Turkish foreign minister, claimed to have evidence that the United States was encouraging Turkey to undertake military action in the eventuality of an Iranian attack against Kirkuk and the pipeline. Such a move would prevent Iran and possibly Syria from occupying the area and thus depriving Turkey, a NATO ally of the United States, of its use.

Most observers, however, felt that such Turkish action was highly unlikely given Turkey's vulnerable frontier with the Soviet Union, serious problems with Greece, and continuing occupation of northern Cyprus, not to mention the certain opposition of both Syria and Iran. Nevertheless, if the Gulf War suddenly had taken a disastrous turn for Iraq, as many for long predicted, the Mosul-Kirkuk area would have become a rich, strategic, political, and economic vacuum that might well have drawn in the Turks. In the event, of course, Iraq did not collapse, and with the end of the war in the summer of 1988, the entire question became moot.

## Western Europe

In recent years a Kurdish diaspora of some 500,000 has formed in western Europe due to a variety of political, economic, sociological, and educational factors. Over 400,000 Kurds now live in West Germany, 60,000 in France, 10,000 in Sweden, 5,000 in Belgium, and others in Britain, the Netherlands, and Italy. Turkish sources have complained that "various extremist organizations and the PKK have used European territory as their play-ground, recruiting new militants, establishing liaison with the East Bloc, transferring militants to Turkey, etc."[24]

Indeed the Socialist Government in France has helped to establish and fund the Kurdish Institute in Paris whose Director is the Turkish Kurd, Kendal Nezan. The Swedish Government has given official recognition to the Kurdish National Union and helped to finance the publication of over twenty books for adults and children in Kurdish. The Swedes also have permitted the establishment of associations for Kurdish teachers, doctors, and writers. From January 13-15, 1989, Stockholm hosted a policy-setting conference of nine Kurdish organizations (including Tevger) from eight different European states.

In June 1987, the European Parliament passed what was considered to be a strongly anti-Turkish resolution "On a political solution to the Armenian Question." Not only taking the Armenian side on this issue, the Parliament went on to chastise the Turks for their Kurdish problem, as well as many other alleged sins: "The European Parliament . . . believes that the refusal by the present Turkish Government to acknowledge the Genocide against the Armenian people . . . and the denial of the existence of the Kurdish question . . . are insurmountable obstacles to consideration of the possibility of Turkey's accession to the [European Economic] Community."[25]

When the Pinarcik attack by the PKK occurred (in which some thirty civilians were murdered as detailed in Chapter 6 above) just two days after this resolution was passed, Turkish President Evren, with some merit, accused the European Parliament of having encouraged the PKK's actions. In truth, however, what probably best explains the gratuitous, anti-Turkish action of the Parliament and its erection of what it termed "insurmountable obstacles" to Turkey's membership in the EEC, was the desire to keep Turkey out of that organization for economic reasons.

Manifesting a militancy that until now had been rare outside of their traditional homeland, groups of Kurds briefly occupied Turkish offices in West Germany and the Netherlands, and the Iraqi Airways office in Paris during the autumn of 1986. The following March Kurdish groups occupied a number of Turkish Airlines offices in various west European cities and demonstrated in front of numerous other offices.[26] Summing up the situation, Siyamend Othman, an official of the Kurdish Institute in Paris, France, wrote: "It is my personal opinion (and fear too) that this [traditional Kurdish quiescence] might not remain the case for much longer since the interviews I have conducted with the leaders and cadres of Kurdish organizations incline me to think that the Kurds, particularly those of Turkey, are beginning to get desperate for attention."[27]

Indeed an underground conflict among Turkish Kurds in western Europe has apparently left at least twenty persons dead in recent years.[28] According to the police, the bloodshed has been caused by the PKK, many of whose supporters have been living in exile in western Europe since the Turkish military coup of September 1980. The violence seems to be aimed at eliminating defectors, attacking ideological foes, and striking at collaborators. A number of violent incidents have occurred at *Newroz* celebrations. For several years nine Turkish Kurds were held in Sweden under what was termed "commune arrest" because of killings there in 1984 and 1985.

Because of this situation, Sweden labeled the PKK a "terrorist organization" in 1984 and refused entry to its leader, Abdullah Ocalan. Nevertheless its members were allowed to remain in the country, while Huseyin Yildirim, until recently the PKK spokesman in western Europe, continued to live in Stockholm.

Following the assassination of Swedish Prime Minister Olof Palme on February 28, 1986, Stockholm Chief of Police Hans Holmer was convinced that it was the work of the PKK. Various motives, some rather bizarre, were offered. Most plausible was that the Swedish government, as mentioned above, had branded the PKK a "terrorist organization" and denied its leader an entry visa. Another claimed that Palme had been working on a secret plan that envisaged autonomy for the Kurds in Turkey. He had been killed because he had asked for some concessions from the PKK which amounted to the Kurds falling under a Swedish mandate.[29] Still another claimed that Iran had paid a large sum of money to the PKK to do the deed because Palme had opposed arms sales to Iran.[30]

Several PKK members were arrested in January 1987 in connection with the murder, but released shortly afterwards due to lack of evidence. Indeed the reputed PKK scenario seemed most far-fetched because Palme was a well-known supporter of such causes as that of the Kurds. Even more, of course, to assassinate a statesman of the stature of the Swedish Prime Minister would obviously backfire in terms of the Kurdish cause. To use the PKK's own terminology, murdering Palme inherently would not be a successful act of armed propaganda.

The arrest of a common Swedish criminal for the deed--followed by his conviction, but then eventual release on appeal--has only served further to confuse the issue. In retrospect the accusations against the PKK smack of a disinformation campaign (possibly by the Turks) to smear the PKK, not totally dissimilar to the one carried out by others that sought to blame the Soviets for the attempted assassination of the Pope in 1981.

In June 1987, the West German Interior Ministry issued a report which stated: "The orthodox communist Kurdish Workers' Party (PKK) was in 1986 by far the most active and most militant extremist organization among the Kurds." The report added that in a publication in West Germany the previous year, the PKK had referred to itself as "the force that has taken up the struggle against the fascist Turkish occupation" and declared that it was committed to "revolutionary violence" in pursuing its goals. Six months later, the Federal Criminal Office in Wiesbaden called the PKK "a dangerous organization" and declared that during the previous year (1987) in West Germany it had been "involved with carrying out at least one murder, two attempted murders, three cases of assault, and four other serious incidents, including robbery, blackmail and coercion."[31] The Office also stated that there were at least 1,000 Kurdish extremists in West Germany trying to overthrow the Turkish government. "Although their primary targets are the Turkish government and fellow Turks [Kurds], West German citizens and institutions who cooperate with the Turkish government . . . are also in danger."[32]

A Kurd who felt that such activities discredited the Kurdish cause wrote: "The Palestinians have their Abu-Nidals; the Armenians an Asala, and we, alas, seem to have to cope with [the] PKK."[33] During a crackdown in Cologne in July 1987, West German police rounded up several Kurdish activists and confiscated money and other valuables worth more than $437,000.

In addition the West German authorities claimed that the PKK was operating through legal organizations to provide cover for their illegal activities. As of July 1988, for example, such fronts included, in addition to the ERNK, the Patriotic Kurdish Workers Party, Kurdish Patriotic Women's Union, and Kurdish Revolutionary Youth Union. Indeed, although he was probably exaggerating, Yilmaz Ciftci, a PKK spokesman in Athens, Greece, told the *Cyprus Weekly* that his party's political arm, the ERNK, "is a massive organization with committees for youth, women's and workers' sections and the liberation army."[34] A Turkish report declared that there were PKK branches in the following West German cities: Mainz, Offenbourg, Russelsheim, Olderburg, and Dortmund.[35]

In the spring of 1987, the PKK began to urge Kurdish supporters living in West Germany to donate the clothing, armaments, and communications gear necessary to equip guerrillas. Specific suggestions included overcoats, raincoats, durable sport shoes, hand-knit wool socks, warm gloves of thin material, undershirts of semifine material, nonnylon shirts, binoculars, radio receivers, compasses, bayonets, and cash.[36]

On the other hand the PKK apparently has been falsely accused of the murder of a West German consular affairs attache, Siegfried Wielsputz, who was shot to death in Paris on January 4, 1988. A leaflet denouncing alleged West German mistreatment of the Kurds and signed by the ERNK was found on his body. The ERNK, however, denied responsibility and denounced the murder as a "cowardly act."[37] Siyamend Othman, a Kurdish spokesman, added that "no Kurd of any organization has ever attacked a Western diplomat. We do not think this has anything to do with Kurds." An ERNK spokesman even went so far as to suggest that "the Turkish National Intelligence Organization and the CIA were behind the plot."[38]

Twelve days later a West German charter plane blew up near Izmir, Turkey, killing all sixteen people aboard. Once again the ERNK was supposedly to blame, but as with the Wielsputz and Palme murders, evidence was lacking. It appeared in these cases at least that there was a campaign to discredit the Kurds in general and the PKK in particular.

Despite the opportunities offered by Europe, in October 1988, Ocalan decided to make a complete about-face in his European strategy and denounced Europe as "a battleground for foul-play."[39] Arguing that, "if we saved ourselves there [and] . . . saved also some of our concepts," it was done "with much pain," he asserted that there was no difference between the fate of the Kurds in Turkey and

Europe. In the one they were being assimilated in the Turkish cities, while in the other they were being Europeanized.

The PKK leader declared that Europe's "intention is to corrupt the PKK." He now believed that Europe "will first corrupt the ideological-political-military structure [of the PKK] and then turn the PKK into a tool for their imperialist aims in the region." The intention of the "Brussels Circle" was to protect the territorial integrity of Turkey, a fellow NATO member. The only way for the Kurds to avoid this trap was for all the militants based in Europe to return to the "war-zone," undergo serious party and military training, and struggle against Turkey.

One of the factors that apparently brought on this tirade was what Ocalan saw as an European attempt to pacify the PKK by promising it financial aid and political asylum, if it would "abandon the resistance . . . and create a more moderate organization which could be accepted." Even more, as mentioned above in Chapter 6, his former associate in Europe, Huseyin Yildirim, had taken the initiative in trying to establish such a more moderate PKK and indeed was now a rival for the leadership of the Kurds in Europe. In other words Ocalan's denunciation of Europe was simply a tactic in an internal PKK power struggle. Therefore it would seem likely that the PKK will continue to use Europe as a safe house and platform for its programs because of the freedom of association and movement it offers.

## The Soviet Union

The Turks and Russians have been enemies for centuries. Until the creation of the Turkish Republic after World War I, no state had benefitted more than Russia from the decline of what Tsar Nicholas I once referred to as "the sick man of Europe." Hassan Arfa, for example, the Chief of Staff of the Iranian army (1944-1946) and the Iranian Ambassador to Turkey (1958-1961), wrote:

> During the Russo-Turkish wars of 1829 and 1853-55, the Russians tried to bring the Kurds to their side, promising them a kind of autonomy and organizing a Kurdish regiment under Russian officers. In 1877, when the Turkish armies were fighting the Russians around Erzurum and Van, the sons of Badr Khan revolted in the Hakkari, Bhutan and Badinan districts. . . .It seems that such ideas were inculcated in them by the Russians.[40]

Now that Turkey has reversed this decline and stands as a member of the NATO alliance, however, continuing Russian ambitions to reach the Mediterranean and the Middle East's oil through Turkey have to be more subtle. Clandestine support of the Turkish Kurdish separatist organizations either directly or through the Syrians, the main Soviet ally in the Middle East, would be one obvious method to further this longstanding goal.

In February 1985, the trial of several Kurdish guerrillas featured evidence of direct Syrian support for them. At that time it was said that the Syrians were not acting alone but had "the backing and encouragement of a superpower."[41] A Turkish foreign ministry official declared:

> We have good reason to believe that the Russians are paying the bill for these guerrillas. It is easy for their agents to find a few hundred unemployed young men who will do this kind of thing for the sake of adventure. It only costs a few million dollars a year. They use the so-called Kurdish Labor Party as a front. It has a completely Marxist program. They can't foment terrorism anywhere else in Turkey now, but in the southeast they can keep the fires burning in the hope of heating them up in the future.[42]

One PKK defendant, Abdurrahoman Kandemir, told a martial law court in Diyarbakir: "Our aim is to establish a Communist Kurdish state. This state is to be a member of the Warsaw Pact."[43] Other PKK members on trial testified about Syrian and Soviet involvement and support for their cause, and of having been trained in Syrian, Iraqi, and Lebanese guerrilla camps.[44]

A report in a prominent American Armenian weekly declared that: "The Syrian intelligence service is providing both haven and assistance to a variety of international terrorists."[45] The account added that: "Heading the list of radical groups now enjoying the protection of the Syrian rulers are the Kurds." All of this "enjoys the indirect support of the Soviet Union, which through its assistance to Syria pursues a policy of destabilizing the region, particularly Turkey."

Under interrogation PKK members have related how Palestinians with Soviet training instructed them in camps under Syrian control after 1980. One account told how a Palestinian, who used the code name "Lt. Abu Haldun," trained PKK members at the Palestinian Cephe Nidal camp. The contact supposedly was facilitated through

the Soviet consulate and cultural center in Damascus.[46]    Nayif
Hawatmeh's Soviet-financed Democratic Front for the Liberation of
Palestine (DFLP) also gave the PKK excellent training facilities at this
time.[47]

Abdulkadir Aygan, a PKK repentant, has spoken about a field
inspection in PKK training camps after 1981 in which the inspectors
were officers from the Soviet Union, Bulgaria, and Cuba.[48] Aygan has
also described his extensive military training in Damascus after his
escape from Turkey in 1982 and his brief stays in southern Cyprus and
Greece.  His roommate at that time was the personal translator of
Ocalan; this individual told Aygan about the PKK leader's routine
meetings with officials from the Soviet consulate in Damascus.  While
interesting, such testimony, of course, is suspect because there usually
is no independent way to verify it.  It also is possible that the
repentant is simply telling his interrogator what he wants to hear in
exchange for leniency.

In a similar vein, therefore, is the testimony of Mehmet Emin
Karatay, the former PKK provincial leader in Mardin who was
captured by security forces on March 10, 1989.[49]  He has told officials
that several Syrian representatives and diplomats from Eastern Bloc
states based in Damascus participated as guests when the PKK
recently held military exercises in the Bekaa Valley.  He also declared
that the Soviet Union had put pressure upon Syria not to honor its
protocol of July 1987 with Turkey (see above) to prevent PKK raids
from Syrian territory.

> We were being transported by Soviet trucks to the Turkish border.
> Suddenly the trucks were stopped by Syrian patrols and we were
> detained.  Ocalan received news of our detention and immediately
> contacted the Soviet officials.  In 24 hours, we were released and
> helped to infiltrate into Turkey.

The CIA Report of the Kurdish problem and what role the
Soviets have played was more circumspect.  "The Soviet-Kurdish
relationship, if tenuous, is relatively old."  The Soviets "probably first
established contact with the Kurds in the early 1920's.  Little resulted,
however."[50]  According to Gwynne Dyer, the Soviets gave financial aid
to the Kurds, among others, through the so-called International
Minority Movement Front in Odessa as early as 1928.[51]  During the
Dersim (Tunceli) revolt in 1937, "it was alleged by the Turkish

government, but never satisfactorily established, that arms had been supplied to the Kurdish rebels by the Soviet Union."[52]

In 1958, the Soviets started a clandestine radio station, *Bazim Radyo* (Our Radio) which broadcast communist propaganda to Turkey from Romania and East Germany. A second station, "the Voice of the Turkish Communist Party," began broadcasting from East Germany in 1968. Although this radio propaganda was mainly aimed at fomenting discontent among the Turks themselves, the Turkish Kurds were not ignored. This second station's commentary of the day on November 9, 1985, for example, declared that: "The oppression of Turkish Kurdistan is continuing. . . . This means that the CIA, or in other words the United States, is supporting the oppressive and hunger policies being implemented by the fascist and chauvinistic Evren-Ozal dictatorship in Turkish Kurdistan."[53] The station claimed that the US desire to protect its bases in eastern Turkey, "is why the United States is supporting the hunting down of patriots by the dictatorship's forces in Turkish Kurdistan." The commentary concluded that: "The only way to put a stop to these developments is for all patriots and democratic forces, Turks and Kurds, to oppose the dictatorship's special cooperation with the U.S. imperialists."

The Kurdish Republic of Mahabad in 1946 is one of the best examples of the Soviet willingness to use Kurdish nationalism against the territorial integrity of one of the states on its southern boundary, in this case Iran.[54] In 1941, British and Soviet troops had occupied Iran to prevent it from supporting Nazi Germany. After the war this joint occupation was lifted, but the Soviets used their position to encourage an Azerbaijani Republic in northern Iran and the rump Mahabad Kurdish Republic in northwestern Iran. The Soviet intention probably was to divide Iran and in time incorporate some of its lost provinces.

Although a Kurdish nationalist, Qazi Muhammad, the leader of the Mahabad Republic, had been "groomed to assume the leadership of a pro-Soviet Kurdish movement that would be tied to the Communist-nationalist effort in Azerbaijan." The Soviets "promised that military equipment including tanks, cannon, machine guns, and rifles would be sent." In November 1945, the Russians delivered a printing press. "Soon afterwards publications in Kurdish began to appear."

Although there was no communist-style social revolution, "Soviet influence was there . . . its strength related to the calculation by the Kurdish leaders that their cause would be bound to succeed if they anticipated Soviet desires and obeyed the advice of Soviet officials. Collaboration was extended willingly." Soon after the Kurdish Republic was established, "there arrived in Mahabad two consignments of about 5,000 Soviet weapons including rifles, machine guns, and pistols. . . . No tanks or artillery pieces had yet been delivered in spite of previous promises, but in their place the Russians provided 'tank destroyers', bottles of petrol equipped with wicks."

Sensing the weakness of the Mahabad Kurds, the Soviet agent "Ibrahimov preached to them the advantages of Kurdish union with Azerbaijan until such time as the Kurds in Iraq and Turkey could be liberated to make possible the formation of a larger, move viable Kurdish state." Nevertheless in March 1945, "Captain Salahaddin Kazimov of the Soviet army arrived in Mahabad to help organize and train the national Kurdish army." Within a month "nearly all persons connected with the Kurdish Government or army could at appropriate times appear looking like Soviet officers in khaki with boots, riding breeches, and caps."

Anglo-American pressure eventually forced the Soviets out of Iran, and with the removal of its sponsor, the Mahabad Republic quickly collapsed. Qazi Muhammad was hanged, while the rump state's military leader, the Iraqi Kurd , Mulla Mustafa Barzani, managed to escape to the Soviet Union. "Red" Mulla, as he was then called, lived there in exile from 1947-1958, and seemed to be proof of the Soviets' willingness to exploit Kurdish nationalism for their own purposes.

In the late 1950s, however, Barzani was allowed to return to Iraq where in time he led a lengthy rebellion with considerable, but indirect *American* aid tendered through Iran because the United States sought to chasten Iraq. This Kurdish insurrection was only terminated when the United States reversed its policy and influenced the Shah to stop supporting the Iraqi Kurds in 1975.[55] Nevertheless, when Barzani died in the United States in 1979, he was seen by some as an agent of U.S. imperialism.

Although used by both, Barzani, of course, was neither a stooge of the Soviets nor the Americans. Rather he was a traditional, tribal Kurdish nationalist leader who took aid from whatever source he could. The American willingness to use and then drop Kurdish nationalism in his case illustrates how the Soviets have no monopoly on this score.

At the present time Kurdish sources argue that the United States opposes Kurdish nationalism in Turkey because Turkey is a valuable US ally and member of NATO. As such, Turkey provides radar stations and large military installations near the Soviet border. These bases have become all the more important for the United States now that the Iranian alliance has been lost. Furthermore Turkey's southern border with Syria is important for detecting Syrian military movements against Israel.[56]

Similarly the Soviets are often tempted to support the Kurds in Turkey and elsewhere as a method ultimately to weaken the United States, as well as promote their own expansion southward. The Soviets must be cautious, however, so as not to antagonize the governments in Ankara, Baghdad, and Tehran with which the Soviets have important relations to protect. Sarcastically, therefore, "many Kurdish intellectuals are beginning to compare the Soviet Union to a doctor whose interests require the patient (Kurdistan) to remain alive but not completely cured so that he may be used one day for research."[57] Indeed Archie Roosevelt, Jr. tells how, because of past memories of Russian and Soviet depredations, "Kurds . . . still frighten their crying children into silence by threatening them with the word 'Russian.'"[58]

The CIA Report concluded that, as of 1979 at least:

> while the Soviets have aided the Kurds occasionally in the past, there is no evidence that they are currently doing so. Indeed, Moscow has done its best to stay aloof of the present round of Kurdish unrest. In any event, since the early 1970s, Soviet state-to-state relations with all the countries involved have consistently taken precedence over the needs and interests of the Kurds. . . . Despite claims in the Turkish press . . . Moscow has been careful to distance itself from the Kurdish separatism.[59]

Similarly a joint appeal by the Socialist Party of Turkish Kurdistan (SPTK) and the Patriotic Union of Kurdistan (PUK) in Iraq declared:

> It is also high time, for all that are interested and concerned with the Kurdish question to divorce themselves from the absurd extreme notions of seeing communism and the Soviet Union, on the one hand, and CIA and U.S. backing, on the other, behind every movement in Kurdistan. A much more balanced and objective analysis can be achieved by concentrating on the indigenous factors,

by scrutinising practices and policies of the respective regimes, and by considering it as an independent phenomenon, instead of always searching for foreign hands behind the scenes.[60]

This, of course, does not mean that the Soviets would fail to fish in troubled waters. As the CIA Report warned: "Should Turkey enter a period of economic and political instability, Moscow might be tempted to try to exploit the Kurdish issue . . . but it would act only with extreme caution."[61] Coming as it does from the intelligence service of its superpower rival, this CIA assessment constitutes strong evidence that the Soviets are probably not the key factor behind the current Kurdish guerrilla war in Turkey some argue they are. Given the remarkable demise of communist rule in eastern Europe during the fall of 1989 and its liberalization in the Soviet Union itself, this conclusion would seem all the more likely to be valid, at least for the present.

## The Armenians

Most observers have considered the Kurds and Armenians to be "inveterate enemies"[62] whose irredentist claims against Turkey are mutually incompatible. Much bloodshed had occurred between the two in the past, and during World War I, the Kurds, who suffered terribly themselves, played a notorious role in the Armenian massacres. As a result, G. R. Driver, the noted English authority, went so far as to conclude, immediately after that War, that an independent Armenia would lead to "a war of extermination between the two races as neither will submit to the yoke of the other."[63] Nevertheless, if for no other reason than their sharing of a common enemy (Turkey), an alliance between the two is not inconceivable today. The purpose of this section is to analyze traces of this collaboration.

During the Paris Peace Conference ending World War I, the Kurdish delegation headed by General Sharif Pasha and the Armenian delegation led by Boghos Nubar Pasha agreed to cooperate. The two presented a joint proposal for a Kurdish and an Armenian state whose exact borders remained to be determined. The Kemalist revival of Turkey, however, frustrated their plans.

In August 1927, the Armenian Revolutionary Federation (the Dashnaks)[64] sent an agent, Vahan Papazian, to Lebanon. There he participated in the foundation of Khoybun, a new Kurdish nationalist organization which eventually launched a major Kurdish uprising in the area of Mt. Ararat under General Ihsan Nuri Pasha. This Kurdish rebellion in Turkey was crushed completely in 1930, but only after the Turks had had to take very great exertions. The observations of Abdul Rahman Ghassemlou, the late Secretary-General of the Kurdistan Democratic Party of Iran (KDPI), on this matter are especially interesting.

> An explanation should be given as to why Dashnaktsutyum supported the Khoiboun. The chief reason was that the Dashnakyans themselves were not capable of organizing any armed movement on Turkish territory and therefore made use of the revolt of the Kurdish population directed against Turkey, whom the Dashnakyans regarded a sworn enemy. . . . Besides, the Dashnakyans supported the Kurdish revolt, hoping it would weaken Turkey and create a suitable opportunity for the future struggle of the Armenians. In case an independent Kurdish state were formed, new prospects would arise for the future struggle of Dashnaktsutyum both against Turkey and against the U.S.S.R. The independent Kurdish state was to become a base of the Dashnakyans for creating a great and independent Armenia.[65]

During this era, Mevlanzade Rifat acted as the liaison between the Kurds in Khoybun and the Armenians. This individual was the Kurdish author of an anti-Turkish, propagandistic account of an apocryphal Young Turk meeting in 1915 where a decision was supposedly taken to exterminate the Armenians.[66] Presumably such "revelations" would facilitate an Armenian-Kurdish alliance. A certain Dr. Tutunjian, the head of the Dashnaks' Central Committee in Syria, served as Rifat's Armenian counterpart.[67] In addition, as noted above, the Soviet-sponsored International Minority Movement Front in Odessa gave financial aid to the Armenians, Kurds, and anti-Kemalists Turks in 1928.[68]

In the current era, association between the Kurds and the Armenians has taken the form of a "declaration" of cooperation between the PKK and the Armenian Secret Army for the Liberation of Armenia (ASALA) which was announced in a press conference in Sidon, Lebanon on April 6, 1980.[69] ASALA members reportedly joined PKK guerrillas and other Kurdish groups when they fought against Turkish troops trying to rout them out from their northern Iraqi sanctuary in May 1983 and again in October 1984.[70]

Commenting on this seemingly anomalous Armenian-Kurdish cooperation, *The Economist* speculated: "It may be that a tactical alliance between Kurds and Armenians, said to have been concluded some three years ago, is in operation on the ground. . . . Armenian brains and world-wide links combined with Kurdish military experience would produce a formidable guerrilla liberation movement."[71]

At approximately the same time a Dashnak theoretical analysis of the "Armenian National Liberation Movement" declared that "the Armenians, the Kurds, and the Palestinians" were "examples" of a "National Liberation Movement."[72]  Monte Melkonian, a dissident ASALA leader, stated in an interview that "to re-establish the political line of the [Armenian] struggle," he envisaged "forging alliances with certain liberation movements, notably in Turkey and with Kurds."[73] The so-called "Armenian World Congress" asserted in 1983 that to "combat . . . Turkish colonialism" it was "necessary to forge an alliance between the Armenian and Kurdish peoples."[74]  Similarly Patrick Devedjian, a well-known French Armenian lawyer who has defended many of the Armenians accused of killing Turkish diplomats in France and was elected to the National Assembly in 1986, stated that the Armenians can start "another Vietnam. . . . The Turkish border is very permeable. . . . This could mean an alliance with Kurds."[75]

For their part "various" Kurdish groups based in Britain expressed their desire 'to collaborate' with Armenian militants against Turkey" in a conference held in London in May 1985.[76]  Celal Talabani, the leader of the Patriotic Union of Kurdistan (PUK), stated in October 1988, that: "Concrete cooperation exists between the Kurds and the Armenians at the present time."  Using the phrase "rapprochement between the Kurds and the Armenians," the Iraqi Kurdish leader added: "We have decided to continue our struggle in a joint way in the future. . . . We now have very close relations with all the Armenian organizations in the world."[77]

In the summer of 1987, the Turkish press claimed that ASALA combatants were among the PKK guerrillas who recently had carried out murderous raids in the Mardin area.  Some of the attackers reportedly had spoken in Armenian.  One Turkish villager was even quoted as saying: "I am almost certain Kurds led the assault and left to Armenians to massacre the innocent villagers."[78]  The following spring it was reported that the PKK was recruiting Syrian Armenians for communications purposes so that they could use the Armenian language for secret messages.[79]

Given the paucity of results over the past decade, however, one must tentatively agree with the dissident ASALA leader Monte Melkonian's assessment that claims to have achieved Armenian-Kurdish cooperation have been "more . . . a tactical ploy than strategic alliance."[80] Indeed Armenian terrorist attacks against Turkish interests stopped in the mid-1980s, and ASALA itself apparently disbanded after a serious of murderous internal splits.[81] This assessment, of course, does not preclude the distinct possibility that ASALA combatants did support the PKK in the early 1980s and that certain Armenians living in Syria and Lebanon probably still do.

### The United States

The United States has been the main ally of Turkey since the late 1940s when the Truman Doctrine helped Turkey to stand up to the Soviet threat against the Straits and northeastern Anatolia. Over the years this close alliance has successfully weathered several crises. The present Kurdish problem in Turkey, however, has threatened to create new difficulties between the two allies.

During the Gulf War some Turkish officials felt that the United States "might also be involved in one way or another"[82] with the PKK insurgency. The argument was made that PKK destabilization activities along Turkey's southeastern border "would eventually force Turkey into the Gulf War or at least ease its attitude in face of the use of bases for this. Thus America too is seen among the countries which benefit out of separatist activities."

A number of other theories also have been suggested for explaining the reputed support of the United States for the Kurds.[83] (1) The US "seeks an autonomous Kurdish state which it could use as a base for Rapid Deployment Forces." (2) To prevent a possible Soviet advance into the Kurdish region, "America may believe that it is necessary to create a natural barrier, a barrier of flesh, made up of Kurdish recruits." (3) The US is trying to divide Turkey so that it can take "control of its overall economic and political mechanism." Although these theories may sound paranoid to most Americans, many reputable Turks seem honestly to believe that "Washington is openly playing a game which endangers Turkey's domestic security and sovereignty in the southeast region."

Several other actions by the United States have further fueled this sentiment. In February 1988, for example, the Turks complained that a "U.S. State Department" report referred to a Kurdish minority in Turkey, while also criticizing that state for the human right violations it had committed against it.[84] This was followed by what many Turks referred to as the "Schifter Blunder," for Richard Schifter, the Assistant Secretary of State for Human Rights and Humanitarian Affairs. According to Turkish sources, Schifter "went out of his way . . . to prove that the Kurds were a different population from the Turks, linguistically and culturally," when he declared: "We believe that although they [the Kurds] are not included in the Lausanne Treaty, they are a national minority by international standards."[85]

According to the Turks, the visit of the Iraqi Kurdish leader, Celal Talabani, to Washington D.C. on June 9, 1988, "seems to be yet another example of US hypocrisy."[86] Talabani, as noted above in Chapter 6, had just recently signed an accord with the PKK. While in Washington, he met with several officials from the U.S. Departments of State and Defense and held a press conference at the National Press Club where he disclosed that he had discussed Turkey's position against the Kurds with these U.S. officials. He also declared that if Turkey cooperated with Iraq, it would be his right to do so with any other group working against Turkey. He further faulted Turkey for saying that the PKK was only killing women and children.

The Turkish reaction to Talabani's visit to Washington was bitter. Foreign Ministry spokesman Inal Batu claimed that Ocalan and Talabani "had joined forces under a joint strategy and the latter had been given audience by US State Department officials." *Milliyet* correspondent Mumtaz Soysal saw the visit as U.S. support for an independent Kurdistan in case of a Soviet threat to the Persian Gulf. *Tercuman* foreign relations writer Fahir Armaoglu viewed it as "an indication to the separatists that if they do as told, they will be supported." Oktay Eksi in *Hurriyet* stated that Talabani was "openly an enemy of Turkey" and "an ally of the other side." He wondered what "the real intention of the United States . . . is when it helps Armenian nationalism develop against Turkey and shows interest to Kurdish freedom movements."

### Notes

1. "General Evren on Important Problems," *Outlook* (Istanbul), Oct. 28, 1981.

2. Ilhan Cevik, "Something's Going On in East Turkey," *Turkish Daily News*, Nov. 11, 1985.

3.  "From Gen. Torumtay's Statement," *Briefing*, Aug. 21, 1989, p. 13.

4.  "A More Realistic Approach in the Offing," *Briefing*, Aug. 28, 1989, p. 19.

5.  See M.M. van Bruinessen, *Agha, Shaikh and State: On the Social and Political Organization of Kurdistan* (Utrecht, The Netherlands: University of Utrecht, 1978), pp. 391, 394-95.

6.  See Kendal [Nezan], "Kurdistan in Turkey," in *People without a Country: The Kurds and Kurdistan*, ed. by Gerard Chaliand (London: Zed Press, 1980), pp. 64-65.

7.  Sa'ad Jawad, *Iraq and the Kurdish Question 1958-1970* (London: Ithaca Press, 1981), p. 289.

8.  "Reviving Terrorism: Can It Be Contained?" *Briefing*, July 24, 1989, p. 17.

9.  "Terror in the East--The Massacre and the PKK," *Briefing*, June 29, 1987, p. 11.

10.  "Mr. Yilmaz Comes Back from Damascus 'Satisfied,'" *Briefing*, July 10, 1989, p. 5.

11.  *Hurriyet*, June 13, 1988.

12.  *Briefing*, July 24, 1989, p. 18.

13.  For an analysis see Suha Bolukbasi, "Turkey Copes with Revolutionary Iran," Paper prepared for delivery at the annual meeting of the American Political Science Association, Atlanta, Georgia, Sept. 2, 1989.

14.  Stephen Pelletiere, *The Kurds: An Unstable Element in the Gulf* (Boulder, Colorado: Westview Press, 1984), p. 187.

15.  The following data were taken from *Briefing*, July 24, 1989, pp. 18-19.

16.  *Briefing*, Aug. 28, 1989, p. 14.

17.  This and the following data were taken from "The PKK: Botan Group at Verge of Destruction but Final Solution Still Far Away," *Briefing*, Aug. 14, 1989, p. 18.

18.  *Ibid.*

19.  Bolukbasi, "Turkey Copes with Revolutionary Iran," pp. 15, 13.

20.  The following data were taken from *Briefing*, July 24, 1989, p. 19.

21.  "PKK Survey: Impact of Rural Violence," *Briefing*, Aug. 17, 1987, pp. 6-7.

22.  "Turkey's Kurds and the Gulf War," *Mid East Markets*, Jan. 25, 1988.

23.  The following discussion mainly is based on Ali-Fuat Borovali, "Kurdish Insurgencies, the Gulf War, and Turkey's Changing Role," *Conflict Quarterly*, 7 (Fall 1987), pp. 37-42; Bolukbasi, "Turkey Copes with Revolutionary Iran," pp. 13-18; Martin van Bruinessen, "The Kurds Between Iran and Iraq," *MERIP Reports*, No. 141 (July-Aug. 1986), pp. 14-27; Sam Cohen, "Gulf War Worries Turkey," *Christian Science Monitor*, Oct. 30, 1986, pp. 9, 10; Mehmet Demir, "Turkish Attacks on Kurds Raise Concerns," *The*

*Guardian*, as reprinted in *The Armenian Weekly*, Apr. 11, 1987, p. 2; Elaine Sciolino, "Turks Warn Iran on Cutting Pipeline," *New York Times*, Mar. 16, 1987, p. A3; "Iranian Guards Stage Mini-invasion of Turkey," *Insight*, Sept. 28, 1987, p. 37; and Martin Seiff, "Kurdish Gains in Mideast Seen as Threat to Iraq and Turkey," *Washington Times*, Sept. 7, 1987.

24. Cited in *Briefing*, July 24, 1989, p. 17.

25. Other "obstacles" to Turkey's EEC membership included: (1) the Greek problem, (2) Cyprus, and (3) democratic and religious freedoms in Turkey.

26. See "March: A Month of Kurdish Activism," *The Armenian Weekly*, May 2, 1987, p. 2.

27. Siyamend Othman, personal correspondence to the author dated Mar. 13, 1987.

28. The following discussion is based on Martin van Bruinessen, "Between Guerrilla War and Political Murder: The Workers' Party of Kurdistan," *Middle East Report*, No. 153 (July-Aug. 1988), pp. 41, 46; Alan Cowell, "Kurd Issue Splits Turks Abroad," *International Herald Tribune*, June 16, 1987, p. 4; and Smith Hempstone, "Warlike Kurds at it Again," *Washington Times*, Nov. 28, 1986.

29. *Hurriyet*, Aug. 23, 1988.

30. *Hurriyet*, June 13, 1988.

31. Cited in "Kurdish Separatists Strike Out at West Germany," *The Armenian Reporter*, Jan. 7, 1988, p. 4.

32. *Ibid*.

33. Siyamend Othman, personal correspondence to the author dated July 17, 1987.

34. Cited in "Kurdish Rebel Claims Victory Within Ten Years," *The Armenian Weekly*, Aug. 8, 1987, p. 6.

35. "PKK Survey-III: Planning Ahead for the Cold Season and on . . .," *Briefing*, Aug. 31, 1987, p. 16.

36. See the report in "Adopt a Terrorist," *Insight*, May 25, 1987, p. 39.

37. This and the following citation were taken from Youssef K. Ibrahim, "Bonn Diplomat Is Slain in Paris and Kurdish Tract Is Found on His Body," *International Herald Tribune*, Jan. 5, 1988.

38. Cited in *Cumhuriyet*, Jan. 12, 1987.

39. This and the following citations and data were taken from "Serious Measures Called for in New 'Attack Season,'" *Briefing*, Feb. 27, 1989, pp. 12-13; and "Yildirim, an Agent of Europe," *Briefing*, Mar. 27, 1989, p. 20.

40. Hassan Arfa, *The Kurds: An Historical and Political Study* (London: Oxford University Press, 1966), pp. 23-24.

41. Paul Henze, "Turkish Government Tackles Problem of Kurdish Insurgency," *Christian Science Monitor*, Oct. 30, 1985, p. 8.

42. *Ibid*.

43. Cited in Emil Anil, "Kurdish Independence Struggle Goes On," *Gulf Daily News*, Aug. 12, 1985.

44. *Ibid.*

45. This and the following citations were taken from "Turks Claim Syrians Actively Assisting Terrorists from Many Lands, Nationalities," *The Armenian Reporter*, Aug. 18, 1983, pp. 1, 2.

46. *Briefing Study*. See note 3 in Chapter 5 for an explanation of this source.

47. Bruinessen, "Workers' Party of Kurdistan," p. 42.

48. *Briefing Study*.

49. The following data and citation were taken from *Briefing*, July 24, 1989, p. 18.

50. National Foreign Assessment Center (US Central Intelligence Agency), *The Kurdish Problem in Perspective* (Aug. 1979), p. 85.

51. Gwynne Dyer, "Correspondence," *Middle Eastern Studies*, 9 (1973), p. 382.

52. Edgar O'Ballance, *The Kurdish Revolt: 1961-1970* (Hamden, Conn.: Archon Books, 1973), p. 29.

53. "Voice of the Turkish Communist Party Denounces Henze Article on 'Turkish Kurdistan,'" *Foreign Broadcast Information Service*, Nov. 9, 1985 (TA091445). This and the following citations were taken from this source. *Bazim Radyo* was closed down on June 11, 1989.

54. The best source on the Mahabad Republic is probably William Eagleton, Jr., *The Kurdish Republic of 1946* (London:  Oxford University Press, 1963).  Also see Archie Roosevelt, Jr., "The Kurdish Republic of Mahabad," *Middle East Journal*, 1 (July 1947), pp. 247-69.  The following citations were taken from Eagleton's analysis.

55. For a report (an edited version of the US Congressional Pike Report) highly critical of the US role here, see "The CIA Report the President Doesn't Want You to Read," *The Village Voice*, Feb. 16, 1976, pp. 70, 85-87.  Also see Ismet Sheriff Vanly, "Kurdistan in Iraq," in *People without a Country:  The Kurds and Kurdistan*, ed. by Gerard Chaliand (London:  Zed Press, 1980), pp. 184 ff.

56. On these points see Chahin Baker, "The Kurdish Question and the Lack of Outside Support," *Kurdish Times*, 1 (Spring 1986), p. 28.

57. *Ibid.*

58. Roosevelt, "Kurdish Republic of Mahabad," pp. 263-64.

59. *Kurdish Problem in Perspective*, pp. 80, 86.

60. The Socialist Party of Turkish Kurdistan and the Patriotic Union of Kurdistan (Iraq), "Appeal:  A Joint Appeal by the People of Kurdistan to the Fortieth Session of the General Assembly of the United Nations," [1985], p. 5.

61. *Kurdish Problem in Perspective*, p. 87.

62. G.R. Driver, *Kurdistan and the Kurds* (Mount Carmel: G. S. I. Printing Section, [1919], p. 97.

63. *Ibid.*

64. The Dashnaks were founded as a nationalist, revolutionary Armenian party in 1890. Over the years they have taken a leading role in the Armenian struggles against the Turks. During the 1970s and 1980s, the Dashnaks turned to terrorism, sponsoring such organizations as the Justice Commandos of the Armenian Genocide from 1975-1983, and the Armenian Revolutionary Army from 1983-1985. For an analysis see Michael M. Gunter, *"Pursuing the Just Cause of Their People": A Study of Contemporary Armenian Terrorism* (Westport, Conn.: Greenwood Press, 1986), pp. 55-65; and Michael M. Gunter, "The Armenian Dashnak Party in Crisis," *Crossroads*, (No. 26, 1987), pp. 75-88.

65. Abdul Rahman Ghassemlou, *Kurdistan and the Kurds* (Prague: Czechoslovak Academy of Sciences, 1965), p. 54.

66. See Mevlanzade Rifat, *Turkiye Inkilabinin Ic Yuzu* [The Hidden Face of the Turkish Revolution] (Aleppo, 1929); and the penetrating critique of this work in Gwynne Dyer, "Turkish 'Falsifiers' and Armenian 'Deceivers': Historiography and the Armenian Massacres," *Middle Eastern Studies* 12 (January 1976), p. 101; and Dyer, "Correspondence," pp. 379-82.

67. See Yves Ternon, *The Armenian Cause* (Delmar, New York: Caravan Books, 1985), p. 102.

68. Dyer, "Correspondence," p. 382.

69. ASALA was a notorious, left-wing Armenian terrorist group that was responsible for numerous bombings and murders of Turkish officials and citizens, as well as others, during 1975-1984. It had ties to radical Palestinians such as Abu Nidal and George Habash, as well as Syria. For an analysis see Gunter, *"Pursuing the Just Cause"*, pp. 41-54. This and the following data were taken from a dissident ASALA source, "Booklet Giving History of ASALA's Existence Gives New Insight into the Revolutionary Movement," *The Armenian Reporter*, Jan. 17, 1985, p. 2.

70. See the reports about this joint Kurdish-Armenian cooperation in "Secret Army Indicates a Loss of 22 Members in Border Skirmish," *The Armenian Reporter*, June 16, 1983, p. 1; and "Turkish Military Battling Kurdish Rebels: Government States Armenians Are Fighting Alongside Kurds," *The Armenian Weekly*, Nov. 3, 1984, pp. 1, 12. Also see claims that "Syria has recently trained Armenian and Kurdish rebels in a joint camp. . . . The two ethnic groups are fighting together now." Uli Schetzer, "Ethnic Kurd Population Persists in Guerrilla War," *International Herald Tribune*, June 8-9, 1985.

71. "The Common Enemy," *The Economist*, June 18, 1983, pp. 55-56.

72. Ara Ashagan, "National Liberation Movements," *The Armenian Weekly*, June 22, 1985, p. 15.

73. "Monte Melkonian Explains His Break with ASALA; Interview," *The Armenian Reporter*, Jan. 12, 1984, p. 4.

74. Armenian World Congress, *Official Documents of Second World Armenian Congress* (Lausanne: Armenian World Congress, 1983), p. 24.

75. Florence Avakian, "Exclusive Interview: French-Armenian Activist & Lawyer Patrick Devedjian Speaks on the Armenian Question," *The Armenian Reporter*, June 6, 1985, p. 2.

76. Mehmet Ogutcu, "Separatists Gang Up in London," *Turkish Daily News* (International Edition), May 10-16, 1985, p. 1.

77. Cited in *Hurriyet*, Oct. 10, 1988.

78. "Turks Claim ASALA Combatants Fighting Alongside Kurd Separatists," *The Armenian Reporter*, July 30, 1987, p. 1. ASALA itself has called for "a Common Front in the region of the Eastern Mediterranean to counter-act the aggressive Turkish expansionist policy." "World Conference on the Armenian Question and Turkish Expansionism," *Armenia* (ASALA organ), No.138; 16, 7th, 1987, p. 1.

79. *Tercuman*, Apr. 8, 1988.

80. Cited in *The Armenian Reporter*, Jan. 17, 1985, p. 2.

81. For an analysis of these events see Michael M. Gunter, *Transnational Armenian Activism* (London: Research Institute for the Study of Conflict and Terrorism, 1990).

82. This and the following citation were taken from *Briefing*, Aug. 17, 1987, pp. 6-7.

83. The following discussion and citations were taken from "US Support for Kurds Annoys Ally," *Briefing*, June 20, 1988, p. 14.

84. The Turks apparently were referring to U.S., Congress, House, Committee on Foreign Affairs, and Senate, Committee on Foreign Relations, *Country Reports on Human Rights Practices for 1987*, 100th Cong., 2d sess., 1988.

85. Cited in *Briefing*, June 20, 1988, p. 12.

86. The following discussion is based on *ibid.*, pp. 11-14.

# 8

## Conclusion

Since its birth in the early 1920s, the Turkish Republic has perceived Kurdish national awareness as a mortal threat to its own territorial integrity. This position was set by the Republic's founder, Mustafa Kemal Ataturk. Given this legacy, Turkey's rulers have been committed to the eradication of practically anything suggestive of a separate Kurdish identity within their country. Even the Kurdish language, as noted above, has been constitutionally "prohibited by law" for use "in the expression and dissemination of thought."[1] During the 1970s and 1980s, Dr. Ismail Besikci, a Turkish sociologist and possibly the *cause celebre* of the cases dealing with the suppression of the Turkish Kurds, spent more than a decade in prison for maintaining in his scholarly work that the Kurds constitute a separate, ethnic group.

The U.S. Department of State has described the situation in the following words:

> Although millions of Turkish Kurds are fully integrated into the political, economic, and social life of the nation, the [Turkish] Government's pursuit of full assimilation has led to the proscription of publications of any book, newspaper, or other material in the Kurdish language. Neither are materials dealing with Kurdish history, culture, and ethnic identity permitted, and there have been instances of arrests of entertainers for singing songs or performing in Kurdish. . . . The foregoing limits on cultural expression are a source of genuine discontent to many Turks of Kurdish origin, particularly in the economically less developed southeast, where they are in the majority.[2]

In August 1984, the *Partia Karkaren Kurdistan* (PKK) or Kurdish Workers Party led by Abdullah (Apo) Ocalan resurrected its guerrilla war of independence in southeastern Turkey that had supposedly been smashed by the Turkish military after it had come to power in September 1980. Despite repeated, subsequent claims that this PKK insurgency had been brought under control, clashes continued to occur on an almost daily basis. By the summer of 1989, they had escalated to such a degree that the Turkish military felt compelled to issue an unprecedented "Statement" concerning the gravity of the matter.

The civilian population in southeastern Anatolia has been trapped between the forces of the state and the insurgents. "The guerrillas have been ruthless in their attacks against civilians who refuse to cooperate with them" reported the Helsinki Watch Committee, at the same time adding that "the Turkish army, on the other hand, is terrorizing the local population, often accusing them indiscriminately of aiding the terrorists."[3] The result, concluded the same organization, is that "much of the southeast seems to be under a continual state of siege."[4] Further reports indicate that the civilian Kurdish population in Turkey is suffering from many other official problems including numerous legal abuses that include torture, forced migrations, forcibly changed names, and a continuing ban on the Kurdish language and culture.[5]

On the other hand Turkish officials point out that many of these legal problems are not unique to the Kurds. Given the internal terrorism Turkey suffered from in the late 1970s and the continuing need for national unity and domestic security, extraordinary legal measures are necessary. As Adnan Kahveci, one of Turkish Prime Minister Turgut Ozal's top advisers, pointed out: "If the founders of the [Turkish] Republic had decided that each ethnic group could have its own language . . . Turkey would today be like Lebanon."[6] Even Helsinki Watch has admitted: "Kurds who think of themselves chiefly as Turks appear to be accepted as such. It is the Kurds who strongly identify themselves as Kurds who run into trouble."[7]

By the late 1980s, however, there was an apparent liberalization of the Turkish position. The heretofore unmentionable word "Kurd" has been increasingly employed. One Turkish source even acknowledged that "for the first time in Turkish history--an open reference to the 'Kurdish question' can be seen in news commentaries as well as reports."[8]

One of the most noteworthy examples to date of this new departure for Turkey occurred when a 13-page cover story of the March 15-21, 1987 issue of *Yeni Gundem*, a major Turkish weekly, devoted itself to an analysis of the Kurdish problem in Turkey. Although the magazine was eventually banned, more than 15,000 copies had already been distributed. According to Siyamend Othman, an official of the Kurdish Institute in Paris, France, this publication constituted "an unprecedented event in the annals of the Turkish press!"[9] Othman went on to write:

> Like some of my colleagues who closely follow developments inside Turkey, I cannot help noticing a relative but, in Turkey's case, qualitative change in the attitudes of certain Turkish intellectuals and politicians vis-a-vis the Kurdish Question. These, for the first time in the history of modern Turkey, appear to be *publicly* acknowledging the existence of Kurds and of a Kurdish problem in their country. Some Kurds are arguing that this has been "forced by the gun." Whatever the truth of the matter, it is a development worth monitoring and, in my opinion, should be construed as a positive step towards the genesis of a dialogue, the only alternative to bloodshed, between the two peoples.[10]

One must caution against too optimistic of an interpretation of these halting steps, however. The liberalization cited above has not altered the official Turkish stress on social-economic conditions and foreign interference, as the two causes of and keys to solving the problem.

There, of course, can be no doubt that southeastern Turkey suffers from serious problems of economic underdevelopment. The CIA Report, for example, stated that "the eastern provinces have received only 10 percent of state industrial investment and only 2 percent of all commercial investments."[11] What is more hospitals and educational facilities are thinly spread in the East. Unemployment is well above the national average. Illiteracy in Turkish among the Kurds is as high as 80 percent; and electricity, piped water, and passable roads are non-existent in more than half of the villages.[12] This is why a vigorous program of economic development for southeastern Turkey is perceived by Turkish officials to be so necessary. Accordingly much hope is being held for the new Ataturk Hydroelectric Dam near Urfa on the Euphrates River. When completed sometime in the 1990s, it is projected to be able to irrigate

1.73 million acres of land, most of which is inhabited by the Turkish Kurds.

In addition it is also clear that the PKK has received invaluable help from such foreign states as Syria. Indeed, without its Syrian safehouse after 1980, it is likely that the PKK would have never been resurrected as it was in 1984. As analyzed above in Chapter 7, a number of other transnational influences have also been present.

While valid points, however, the official Turkish stress on socio-economic conditions and foreign help continues to ignore the main reason for the Kurdish problem in Turkey, the official cultural suppression of the Kurds. As the Turkish writer, Aziz Nesin, declared at a meeting in Ankara in May 1989: "If these people cannot even say that they are Kurds and if they are being forced to accept the historical thesis saying they are Turks, there is no way to put democracy into practice in this country."[13]

What then can be done? The PKK has succeeded in calling the Kurdish problem in Turkey to the attention of the world. Given the relative power of Turkey and its determination to defend its territorial integrity, however, it is not likely that the PKK will be able to achieve its ultimate goal of establishing an independent Kurdistan in south-eastern Anatolia. Does this mean, therefore, that, as a senior Turkish military commander has warned: "We must accept realities and be prepared for a long struggle. This is like the situation which the British face with the IRA and the Spaniards with the ETA [Basque] separatists"?[14]

This negative prognostication does not have to materialize if the Turkish government is able to manifest a greater sense of maturity and self-confidence. As Turkish Prime Minister Turgut Ozal cryptically responded in September 1989 to a question about the existence of a Kurdish minority in Turkey: "If in the first years of the Republic, during the single-party period, the State committed mistakes on this matter, it is necessary to recognise these."[15] If the authorities now could bring themselves no longer to see expressions of Kurdish cultural awareness as a mortal threat to the continuing existence of the territorial integrity of Turkey, it is likely that the disaffected Kurdish elements in that state could learn to accept their role as loyal Turkish citizens. Comments made by the Iraqi Kurdish leader, Celal Talabani, at the end of 1988 give some credence to this argument:

Compared with that of Kurds in other countries, the situation for Kurds in Turkey is much better. This was due to the "semidemocratic system" which exists in Turkey. . . . The Kurds have always sided with Turkey in history. They have never abandoned Turkey in bad times.[16]

Talabani went on to argue that the PKK would halt all its activities if a federal Turkey were established and declared: "PKK leader Abdullah Ocalan has been telling me this quite clearly."[17]

What is needed then is the wisdom and strength of an Ataturk who, if he were alive today and thus could see what an impasse his Kurdish policy has led to, would trust more in the permanency of the institutions he had created and fear less the inherent logic of democracy by granting Turkey's citizens of Kurdish ancestry their most elemental cultural rights. This probably does not mean that the proposal of a federal solution as called for by Talabani and Ocalan is necessary, but it does imply, as Erdal Inonu, the leader of the opposition SHP in Turkey and son of Ataturk's closest lieutenant, Ismet Inonu, has stated: "Everyone should express himself without fear in his mother tongue."[18]

Turkey's allies, the United States and the European Economic Community (which Turkey longs to join), should encourage and help Turkey to take these steps. When they finally are, Turkey hopefully will have become stronger both politically (because the Kurdish problem at least will have become more manageable) and economically (as a member of the EEC). In the meantime, while the Turkish government finds a way to permit Kurdish cultural expression within the limits of a unitary Turkish state, it would help if others would be more understanding of the dilemma faced by that state, as well as more willing to grant the positive accomplishments of that state's nationalities policy to date.

### Notes

1.    Article 26 of the present (1982) Turkish Constitution.
2.    U.S., Congress, Senate, Committee on Foreign Relations and House, Committee on Foreign Affairs, *Country Reports on Human Rights Practices for 1988*, 101st Cong., 1st sess., 1989, p. 7.

3.  U.S. Helsinki Watch Committee, *Destroying Ethnic Identity: The Kurds of Turkey* (New York and Washington:   U.S. Helsinki Watch Committee, 1988), p. 29.

4.  *Ibid.*

5.  In addition to the Helsinki Watch and Amnesty International reports cited above in note 53 of Chapter 3, see the following two reports by the Socialist Party of Turkish Kurdistan (SPTK), "Report on the Violation of Human Rights in Turkish-Kurdistan," Apr. 1987; and "Report on the Violations of Human Rights in Turkish-Kurdistan," May 1988.

6.  Adnan Kahveci, "On the Question of Ethnic Problems in Turkey," *Turkish Daily News*, June 2, 1987, p. 6.

7.  *Destroying Ethnic Identity*, p. 7.

8.  "PKK Strikes Again:  The Attacks Will Continue," *Briefing*, Aug. 24, 1987, pp. 13-14.

9.  Siyamend Othman, personal correspondence to the author dated Mar. 25, 1987.

10.  *Ibid.*

11.  National Foreign Assessment Center (U.S. Central Intelligence Agency), *The Kurdish Problem in Perspective* (Aug. 1979), p. 20.

12.  *Ibid.*  For a further analysis of the economic situation in southeastern Turkey see Majeed R. Jafar, *Under-underdevelopment: A Regional Case Study of the Kurdish Area in Turkey* (Helsinki:   Social Policy Association, 1976).

13.  Cited in "Time and Effort Needed to Restore Democracy," *Briefing*, May 9, 1989, p. 12.

14.  Cited in Sam Cohen, "Turkey's Kurdish Campaign Heats Up," *Christian Science Monitor*, Mar. 11, 1987, p. 11.

15.  Cited in "Ozal Puts Up Brave Performance in Strasbourg-But Brussels Still Says 'No,'" *Briefing*, Oct. 2, 1989, p. 4.

16.  Cited in *Hurriyet*, Oct. 10, 1988.

17.  Cited in *Ibid.*

18.  Cited in *Hurriyet*, Feb. 24, 1989.

# Selected Bibliography

For numerous, additional references to specific articles in newspapers, the reader should refer to the notes at the end of each chapter.

## Interviews

Azad, Selim. Official of the Socialist Party of Turkish Kurdistan (SPTK), Stockholm, Sweden, Nov. 1987.

Othman, Siyamend. Official of the Institut Kurde de Paris, Paris, France, Oct. 1986.

Rasul, Kamal. Director of the Kurdish Cultural Centre, London, Britain, Mar. 1989.

Saeedpour, Vera Beaudin. Director of the Kurdish Library, Brooklyn, New York, Aug. 1986, Aug. 1987, Nov. 1987, Aug. 1988, and Oct. 1989.

Vanly, Ismet Sheriff. Kurdish academician, Lausanne, Switzerland, Oct. 1989.

## Correspondence

Othman, Siyamend. Official of the Institut Kurde de Paris, Paris, France. Letters to the author dated Jan. 5, 1987, Mar 13, 1987, Mar. 25, 1987, July 17, 1987, Aug. 10, 1987, and Oct. 27, 1987.

## Documents

### United States

National Foreign Assessment Center (U.S. Central Intelligence Agency) *The Kurdish Problem in Perspective.* Aug. 1979. Throughout the text this source is referred to as the "CIA Report."

United States Congress. "Hearing before the Subcommittee on Security and Terrorism of the Committee on the Judiciary United States Senate on

Turkish Experience with Terrorism." (Testimony of Aydin Yalcin) Serial No. J-97-43, 97th Cong., 1 sess., 1981.

------. House, Committee on Foreign Affairs, and Senate, Committee on Foreign Relations. *Country Reports on Human Rights Practices for 1987.* 100th Cong., 2d sess., 1988.

------. Senate, Committee on Foreign Relations and House, Committee on Foreign Affairs. *Country Reports on Human Rights Practices for 1988.* 101st Cong., 1st sess., 1989.

"Voice of the Turkish Communist Party Denounces Henze Article on 'Turkish Kurdistan.'" *Foreign Broadcast Information Service.* (TA091445) Nov. 9, 1985.


*Turkish*


*Anarchy and Terrorism in Turkey.* (Report issued by the Turkish government, [1982].)

General Secretariat of the [Turkish] National Security Council. *12 September in Turkey: Before and After.* Ankara: Ongun Kardesler Printing House, 1982.



**Kurdish Publications & Documents**

*Azadi Kurdistan Humane Foundation.* South San Francisco, California, Mar., 1986.

Baker, Chahin. "The Kurdish Question and the Lack of Outside Support." *Kurdish Times* 1 (Spring 1986), pp. 27-32.

Baran, Aziz. "You Must Give a Kurdish Baby a Turkish Name." *Kurdish Times* 1 (Spring 1986), pp. 12-15.

Besikci, Ismail. Letter written to Madame Mousse Boulanger, Chairperson of the Swiss Union of Writers. Aug. 14, 1980, translation supplied by Michael Maher.

"Ibrahim Kaypakkaya on the Kurdish National Question." *A World to Win* (Feb. 1986), pp. 14-15, 73-80.

Institut Kurde de Paris. *Information and Liaison Bulletin.* 1983-.

Izady, Mehrdad. "The Question of an Ethnic Identity: Problems in the Historiography of Kurdish Migration and Settlement." *Kurdish Times* 1 (Spring 1986), pp. 16-18.

Jaff, B. "Northern Kurdistan." *The Kurdish Observer* 1 (Feb. 1987), pp. 10-14.

"Kurdistan: A Forgotten Cause." *The Kurdish Observer* 1 (Dec. 1987), pp. 8-9.

"Kurdistan of Turkey." *DRUK* (Defend the Rights of United Kurdistan) Bulletin No. 3, Vol. 1, July 30, 1975.

Lana, Boug. "The Socio-Economic Framework of National Oppression in Kurdistan-Turkey." *The Kurdish Cultural Bulletin* 1 (Nov. 1988), pp. 11-24.

Manuelian, Matthew der. "Resettlement of Central Asian Refugees in the Kurdish Region of Turkey." *Kurdish Times* 1 (Spring 1986), pp. 19-20.

National Liberation Front of Kurdistan [PKK]. "Genocide: After the Armenians, the Kurds." July 1987.

Othman, Siyamend. "The Guney File." *Armenian Review* 37 (Autumn 1984), pp. 45-59.

Saeedpour, Vera Beaudin. "Kurdish Times and the New York Times." *Kurdish Times* 2 (Summer 1988), pp. 25-41.

------. "The Kurdish Way of Life in Turkey." *Kurdish Times* 1 (Spring 1986), pp. 7-11.

Serxwebun [PKK]. "Programme." Feb. 1983.

Siavush, Nejimeh. "Kurdistan and Prospects for Red Political Power." *A World to Win* (Feb. 1986), pp. 5-14.

Socialist Party of Turkish Kurdistan (SPTK). "A Report of the Address by Kemal Burkay, General Secretary of the Socialist Party of Turkey Kurdistan, to the Labour Movement Conference on Turkey Held 22nd September, 1984, at the Headquarters of the NUR." n. d.

------. "Report on the Violation of Human Rights in Turkish-Kurdistan." Apr. 1987.

------. "Report on the Violations of Human Rights in Turkish-Kurdistan." May 1988.

------. "The Socialist Party of Turkish Kurdistan." May 1982.

------. "Socialist Party of Turkish Kurdistan (SPTK), Appeal to the Delegates of the 23rd General Conference of the UNESCO, Sofia/Bulgaria." Oct. 8, 1985.

Socialist Party of Turkish Kurdistan and the Patriotic Union of Kurdistan (Iraq). "Appeal: A Joint Appeal by the People of Kurdistan to the Fortieth Session of the General Assembly of the United Nations." [1985].

"The Trial of Ismail Besikci." *Kurdish Times* 2 (Fall 1986), pp. 5-43.

"Turkey: The Vulture in the Middle Eastern Ruins." *The Kurdish Observer* 1 (Dec. 1987), p. 15.

## Human Rights Reports

Amnesty International. *Amnesty International Report 1983*. London: Amnesty International Publications, 1984.

------. *Continuing Violations of Human Rights in Turkey*. London: Amnesty International Publications, 1987.

------. *Torture in the Eighties*. London: Amnesty International Publications, 1984.

U.S. Helsinki Watch Committee. *Destroying Ethnic Identity: The Kurds of Turkey*. New York and Washington: U.S. Helsinki Watch Committee, 1988.

------. *Freedom and Fear: Human Rights in Turkey*. New York and Washington: U.S. Helsinki Watch Committee, 1986.

------. *Human Rights in Turkey's 'Transition to Democracy'*. New York and Washington: U.S. Helsinki Watch Committee, 1983.

------. *Paying the Price: Freedom of Expression in Turkey*. New York and Washington: U.S. Helsinki Watch Committee, 1989.

------. *State of Flux: Human Rights in Turkey*. New York and Washington: U.S. Helsinki Watch Committee, 1987.

------. *Straws in the Wind: Prospects for Human Rights and Democracy in Turkey*. New York and Washington: U.S. Helsinki Watch Committee, 1984.

------. *Violations of the Helsinki Accords: Turkey*. New York and Washington: U.S. Helsinki Watch Committee, 1986.

### Newspapers, Magazines, etc.

#### Turkish

*Cumhuriyet*, 1987-.
*Hurriyet*, 1988-.
*Milliyet*, 1984-.
*Tercuman*, 1988-.
*Turkish Daily News*, 1984-.
*Turkish Daily News* (International Edition), 1984-.

#### Others

*Arab News*, 1988-.
*Christian Science Monitor*, 1971-.
*Financial Times*, 1986-.
*Gulf Daily News*, 1985-.
*International Herald Tribune*, 1984-.
*Jerusalem Post (International Edition)*, 1987-.
*Le Matin*, 1984-.
*Le Monde*, 1984-.

*Middle East International*, 1983-.
*Mid East Markets*, 1983-.
*New York Times*, 1981-.
*Le Soir*, 1984-.
*Wall Street Journal*, 1984-.
*Washington Post*, 1981-.
*Washington Times*, 1986-.

## Weeklies, Monthlies

*The Armenian Mirror-Spectator*, 1987-.
*The Armenian Reporter*, 1983-.
*The Armenian Weekly*, 1983-.
*Briefing* (Turkey), 1984-.
*Briefing Study*, 1988. This was a detailed analysis of the PKK published by the independent Turkish weekly *Briefing* and written by its diplomatic news editor, Ismet G. Imset, over a period of several weeks in the summer of 1988.
*The Economist*, 1983-.
*Insight*, 1987-.
*Turkey Briefing* (London), 1987-.

## Articles in Popular Journals

"The CIA Report the President Doesn't Want You to Read." *The Village Voice*. Feb. 16, 1976, pp. 70, 85-87.
Kaplan, Robert. "Kurdistan: Sons of Devils." *The Atlantic*, Nov. 1987, pp. 38-44.
"Kurt Sorunu Gundem." *Yeni Gundem* (Turkey), Mar. 15-21, 1987, pp. 10-22.
Liber, Jeri. "Turkey's Nonpeople." *The New York Review*, Feb. 4, 1988, pp. 14-17.
Mackenzie, Ken. "Turkey, Iraq and the Kurds." *Middle East International*, Sept. 23, 1988, pp. 10-11.
"A Remote but Bitter War: Kurds and Turks Fight It Out in the 'Wild East.'" *Newsweek*, Mar. 30, 1987, p. 45.
Sagirsoy, Ilter. "Genelkurmay'in PKK Raporuu." *Nokta* (Turkey), Apr. 8, 1990, pp. 18-24.
Skutel, H.J. "Turkey's Kurdish Problem." *International Perspectives*, Jan.-Feb. 1988, pp. 22-25.

## Scholarly Papers

Bolukbasi, Suha. "Turkey Copes with Revolutionary Iran." Paper prepared for delivery at the annual meeting of the American Political Science Association, Atlanta, Georgia, Sept. 2, 1989.

Gunter, Michael M. "Domestic Violence in Turkey during the 1970s." Paper delivered to the annual meeting of the American Political Science Association, Atlanta, Georgia, Sept. 2, 1989.

------. "The Kurdish Insurgency in Turkey." Paper delivered to the annual meeting of the Middle East Studies Association of North America, Los Angeles, California, Nov. 5, 1988.

------. "Kurdish Militancy in Turkey: The Case of PKK." Paper delivered to the annual meeting of the Middle East Studies Association of North America, Baltimore, Maryland, Nov. 15, 1987.

------. "The Kurdish Problem in Turkey." Paper delivered to the annual meeting of the Middle East Studies Association of North America, Boston, Massachusetts, Nov. 23, 1986.

Olson, Robert W. "Four Stages of Kurdish Nationalism: From Sheikh Ubaydallah to Sheikh Said, 1880-1925." Paper delivered to the annual meeting of the Middle East Studies Association of North America, Los Angeles, California, Nov. 5, 1988.

## Articles in Scholarly Journals

Baksi, Mahmut. "The Immigrant Experience in Sweden." *MERIP Reports*, No. 123 (May 1984), pp. 19-22.

Borovali, Ali-Fuat. "Kurdish Insurgencies, the Gulf War, and Turkey's Changing Role." *Conflict Quarterly* 7 (Fall 1987), pp. 29-45.

Brown, James. "The Politics of Transition in Turkey." *Current History* 87 (Feb. 1988), pp. 69-72.

Bruinessen, Martin van. "Between Guerrilla War and Political Murder: The Workers' Party of Kurdistan." *Middle East Report* No. 153 (July-Aug. 1988), pp. 40-42, 44-46, 50.

------. "The Kurds between Iran and Iraq." *Middle East Report* No. 141 (July-Aug. 1986), pp. 14-27.

------. "The Kurds in Turkey." *MERIP Reports* No. 121 (Feb. 1984), pp. 6-12.

Dyer, Gwynne. "Correspondence." *Middle Eastern Studies* 9 (1973), pp. 379-82.

------. "Turkish 'Falsifiers' and Armenian 'Deceivers': Historiography and the Armenian Massacres." *Middle East Studies* 12 (Jan. 1976), pp. 99-107.

Edmonds, C. J. "Kurdish Nationalism." *Journal of Contemporary History* 6 (1971), pp. 87-107.

Entessar, Nader. "The Kurdish Mosaic of Discord." *Third World Quarterly* 11 (Oct. 1989), pp. 83-100.

Gunter, Michael M. "The Kurdish Problem in Turkey." *Middle East Journal* 42 (Summer 1988), pp. 389-406.

------. "Political Instability in Turkey during the 1970s." *Conflict Quarterly* 9 (Winter 1989), pp. 63-77.

Hale, William M. "The Role of the Electoral System in Turkish Politics." *International Journal of Middle East Studies* 11 (1980), pp. 401-17.

Harris, George S. "Ethnic Conflict and the Kurds." *Annals AAPSS* 433 (Sept. 1977), pp. 112-24.

------. "The Left in Turkey." *Problems of Communism* 29 (July-Aug. 1980), pp. 26-42.

Heinrich, Lothar A. "Die Arbeiterpartei Kurdistan (PKK): Kult des Opfers und Kult der Tat als Programm." *Orient* 29 (No. 3, 1988), pp. 423-39.

Ludington, Nicholas S. and James W. Spain. "Dateline Turkey: The Case for Patience." *Foreign Policy* No. 50 (Spring 1983), pp. 150-68.

Mardin, Serif. "Youth and Violence in Turkey." *European Journal of Sociology* 19 (1978), pp. 229-54.

Roosevelt, Archie, Jr. "The Kurdish Republic of Mahabad." *Middle East Journal* 1 (July 1947), pp. 247-69.

Rustow, Dankwart A. "The Army and the Founding of the Turkish Republic." *World Politics* 11 (July 1959), pp. 513-52.

Steinitz, Mark S. "Insurgents, Terrorists and the Drug Trade." *The Washington Quarterly* (Fall 1985).

Yalcin, Lale. "Ismail Besikci: State Ideology and the Kurds." *Middle East Report* No. 153 (July-Aug. 1988), p. 43.

## Articles in Edited Works

Barkey, Henri. "Crises of the Turkish Political Economy of 1960-1980," in Ahmet O. Evin ed. *Modern Turkey: Continuity and Change.* Opladen: Leske und Budrich, 1984.

Bois, Thomas and Vladimir Minorsky. "Kurds, Kurdistan." *The Encyclopedia of Islam* (new edition), V, 1981, 438-86.

Dumont, Paul. "The Origins of Kemalist Ideology," in Jacob M. Landau ed. *Ataturk and the Modernization of Turkey.* Boulder: Westview Press, 1984, pp. 25-44.

Ghassemlou, A. R. "Kurdistan in Iran," in Gerard Chaliand ed. *People without a Country: The Kurds and Kurdistan.* London: Zed Press, 1980, pp. 107-34.

Gunter, Michael M. "On Turkish Students," in Arthur P. Dudden and Russell R. Dynes eds. *The Fulbright Experience, 1946-1986.* New Brunswick: Transaction Books, 1987, pp. 281-84.

Gurr, Ted Robert. "Psychological Factors in Civil Violence," in I. K. Feierabend *et al.* eds. *Anger, Violence, and Politics.* Englewood Cliffs: Prentice Hall, 1972, pp. 31-57.

Henze, Paul. "Organized Crime and Drug Linkages," in Uri Ra'anan *et al.* eds. *The Hydra of Carnage: International Linkages of Terrorism, The Witnesses Speak.* Lexington: D. C. Heath and Company, 1986, pp. 171-87.

MacDonald, Charles G. "The Kurdish Question in the 1980s," in Milton J. Esman and Itamar Rabinovich eds. *Ethnicity, Pluralism, and the State in the Middle East.* Ithaca: Cornell University Press, 1988, pp. 233-52.

Magnarella, Paul J. "Civil Violence in Turkey: Its Infrastructural, Social and Cultural Foundations," in Cigdem Kagitcibasi ed. *Sex Roles, Family and Community in Turkey.* Bloomington: Indiana University Press, 1982, pp. 383-401.

"Memorandum of the Kurdish Rizgari Party, Baghdad, 18th January 1946," in F. David Andrews ed. *The Lost Peoples of the Middle East: Documents of the Struggle for Survival and Independence of the Kurds, Assyrians, and Other Minority Races in the Middle East.* Salisbury: Documentary Publications, 1982, pp. 87-88.

Minorsky, Vladimir. "Kurdistan." *The Encyclopaedia of Islam*, 1927, 1130-32.

------. "Kurds." *The Encyclopaedia of Islam*, 1927, 1132-55.

[Nezan], Kendal. "Kurdistan in Turkey," in Gerard Chaliand ed. *People without a Country: The Kurds and Kurdistan.* London: Zed Press, 1980, pp. 47-106.

------. "The Kurds under the Ottoman Empire," in Gerard Chaliand ed. *People without a Country: The Kurds and Kurdistan.* London: Zed Press, 1980, pp. 19-46.

Sunar, Ilkay and Sabri Sayari. "Democracy in Turkey: Problems and Prospects," in Guillermo O'Donnell *et al.* eds. *Transitions from Authoritarian Rule: Prospects for Democracy.* Baltimore and London: The Johns Hopkins University Press, 1986.

Vanly, Ismet Sheriff. "Kurdistan in Iraq," in Gerard Chaliand ed. *People without a Country: The Kurds and Kurdistan.* London: Zed Press, 1980, pp. 153-210.

## Booklets and Pamphlets

Besikci, Ismail. *M. Kemal Ataturk: UNESCO and Destruction of Kurdish Identity in Turkey*. Croydon Park, N.S.W.: Committee for Decolonization of Kurdistan, 1986.

Hyman, Anthony. *Elusive Kurdistan: The Struggle for Recognition*. No. 214. London: The Centre for Security and Conflict Studies, 1988.

McDowall, David. *The Kurds*. No. 23. London: Minority Rights Group Ltd., 1985.

Sezer, Duygu Bazoglu. *Turkey's Security Policies*. Adelphi Paper No. 164. London: International Institute for Strategic Studies, 1981.

Short, Martin and Anthony McDermutt. *The Kurds*. No. 23. London: Minority Rights Group, Ltd., 1975.

Sims, Richard. *Kurdistan: The Search for Recognition*. No. 124. London: The Institute for the Study of Conflict, 1980.

## Books

Arfa, Hassan. *The Kurds: An Historical and Political Study*. London: Oxford University Press, 1966.

Barchard, David. *Turkey and the West*. London: Routledge & Kegan Paul for the Royal Institute of International Affairs, 1985.

Berberoglu, Berch. *Turkey in Crisis*. London: Zed Press, 1982.

Besikci, Ismail. *Dogu Anadolu'nun Duzeni: Sosyo-Ekonomik ve Etnik Temeller* [The Order of Eastern Anatolia: Socio-Economic and Ethnic Foundations]. Istanbul: E. Yayinlari, 1970.

Birand, Mehmet Ali. *The General's Coup in Turkey: An Inside Story of 12 September 1980*, trans. by M.A. Dikerdem. London: Brassey's Defence Publishers, 1987.

Bois, Thomas. *The Kurds*, trans. by M. W. M. Welland. Beirut: Khayats, 1965.

Bruinessen, M. M. van. *Agha, Shaikh and State: On the Social and Political Organization of Kurdistan*. Utrecht: University of Utrecht, 1978.

Driver, G. R. *Kurdistan and the Kurds*. Mount Carmel: G. S. I. Printing Section, [1919].

Eagleton, William, Jr. *An Introduction to Kurdish Rugs and Other Weavings*. Brooklyn: Interlink Books, 1988.

------. *The Kurdish Republic of 1946*. London: Oxford University Press, 1963.

Edmonds, C. J. *Kurds, Turks and Arabs: Politics, Travel and Research in North-Eastern Iraq 1919-1925.* London: Oxford University Press, 1957.

Ghareeb, Edmund. *The Kurdish Question in Iraq.* Syracuse: Syracuse University Press, 1981.

Ghassemlou, Abdul Rahman. *Kurdistan and the Kurds.* Prague: Czechoslovak Academy of Sciences, 1965.

Gunter, Michael M. *"Pursuing the Just Cause of Their People": A Study of Contemporary Armenian Terrorism.* Westport: Greenwood Press, 1986.

Gurr, Ted Robert. *Why Men Rebel.* Princeton: Princeton University Press, 1970.

Hale, William M. ed. *Aspects of Modern Turkey.* London: Bowker, 1976.

------. *The Political and Economic Development of Modern Turkey.* New York: St. Martin's Press, 1981.

Harris, George. *Turkey: Coping with Crisis.* Boulder: Westview Press, 1985.

Henze, Paul. *The Plot to Kill the Pope.* New York: Charles Scribner's Sons, 1985.

Herman, Edward S. and Frank Brodhead. *The Rise and Fall of the Bulgarian Connection.* New York: Sheridan Square Publications, 1986.

Heyd, Uriel. *The Foundations of Turkish Nationalism: The Life and Teachings of Ziya Gokalp.* London: Harvil Press, 1950.

Jafar, Majeed R. *Under-underdevelopment: A Regional Case Study of the Kurdish Area in Turkey.* Helsinki: Social Policy Association, 1976.

Jawad, Sa'ad. *Iraq and the Kurdish Question 1958-1970.* London: Ithaca Press, 1981.

Kahn, Margaret. *Children of the Jinn. In Search of the Kurds and Their Country.* New York: Seaview Books, 1980.

Kinnane, Derk. *The Kurds and Kurdistan.* London: Oxford University Press, 1964.

Landau, Jacob M. *Radical Politics in Modern Turkey.* Leiden: E. J. Brill, 1974.

Lewis, Bernard. *The Emergence of Modern Turkey.* London: Oxford University Press, 1968.

O'Ballance, Edgar. *The Kurdish Revolt: 1961-1970.* Hamden: Archon Books, 1973.

Olson, Robert. *The Emergence of Kurdish Nationalism and the Sheikh Said Rebellion, 1880-1925.* Austin: University of Texas Press, 1989.

Ozbudun, Ergun. *The Role of the Military in Recent Turkish Politics.* Cambridge: Harvard University, Center for International Affairs, 1966.

Pelletiere, Stephen. *The Kurds: An Unstable Element in the Gulf.* Boulder: Westview Press, 1984.

Pevsner, Lucille. *Turkey's Political Crisis: Background, Perspectives, Prospects.* New York: Praeger, 1984.

Poppenburg, Walter. *Bucher uber die Kurden und Kurdistan: Eine Auswahl-bibliographie.* Bonn: Verlag fur Kultur und Wissenschaft, 1987.

Rambout, L. *Les Kurdes et le droit.* Paris: Le Cerf, 1947.

Rustow, Dankwart A. *Turkey: America's Forgotten Ally.* New York: Council on Foreign Relations, 1987.

Sterling, Claire. *The Terror Network: The Secret War of International Terrorism.* New York: Holt, Rinehart and Winston, 1981.

------. *The Time of the Assassins: Anatomy of an Investigation.* New York: Holt, Rinehart and Winston, 1983.

Tamkoc, Metin. *The Warrior Diplomats: Guardians of National Security and the Modernization of Turkey.* Salt Lake City: University of Utah Press, 1976.

Ternon, Yves. *The Armenian Cause.* Delmar: Caravan Books, 1985.

Vanly, Ismet Sheriff. *Survey of the National Question of Turkish Kurdistan with Historical Background.* Zurich: Hevra, [1971].

Weiker, Walter. *The Modernization of Turkey: From Ataturk to the Present Day.* New York: Holmes Meier, 1981.

------. *The Turkish Revolution, 1960-1961: Aspects of Military Politics.* Washington: The Brookings Institution, 1963.

Zulkuf, Aydin. *Underdevelopment and Rural Structures in Southeastern Turkey: Gisgis and Kalhana.* London: Ithaca Press, 1986.

# Index